Robert G ...orks f...
claimants at ...ppeal he...   RY
worked for several ve... ...n adviso...
hood advice centr... ...nd a Law Centre
stems from his own experience of cla...

Rick Middleton has worked with CHAR, t... ... less
people, for the past five years. As CHAR's s... ...r, he has given
advice regularly on a range of benefits; prepared su... ...ons to the government
on proposed changes in the law; written and the... revised CHAR's popular
annual 120-page guide to housing and supplementary benefits for homeless
people and boarders. He has recently concluded a de...nitive work explaining
the law, interpretation and problems surrounding supplementary benefit single
payments.

Peter Esam leads Greenwich Council's team of welfare rights officers, working on benefit take-up campaigns, training Council staff and supporting campaigns on benefit issues. He has special responsibility for policy matters,
preparing reports to the Council on advice provision in the borough, on the
level of deprivation and its causes and on the government's social security
reviews. Last year he supervised a major survey of living standards in
Greenwich. He recently completed an M.Sc. in Sociology and Politics at
London University.

Peter Esam
Robert Good
Rick Middleton

Verso

Who's To Benefit?

A Radical Review of the Social Security System

Verso is the imprint of **New Left Books**

British Library
Cataloguing in Publication Data

Esam, Peter
  Who's to benefit?: a radical review of the
  social security system.
  1. Social security — Great Britain
  I. Title   II. Good, Robert   III. Middleton, Rick
  368.4' 00941   HD7165

First published 1985
© Peter Esam, Robert Good and Rick Middleton

Verso
15 Greek Street London W1V 5LF

Typeset in Bembo by
Boldface Typesetters Ltd, London

Printed in Great Britain by
The Thetford Press Ltd
Thetford, Norfolk

ISBN 0 86091 111 X
     0 86091 818 1 Pbk

Contents

Acknowledgements

Very many people have been helpful either by discussing ideas in the book or being generally supportive — particularly friends at home and at work.

We would like to thank especially Suzanne MacGregor who gave advice and commented in detail on the whole text, and the following people who made helpful suggestions about earlier drafts: Andy Candler, Sue Carter, Eileen Edwards, Dick Esam, Brian Hill, Barbara Joel, Linda Lennard and other workers at the Disability Alliance, Emma MacLennon, Barry Powles, Carol Wallicker, Matthew Warburton and Sue Ward.

Thanks also to Central London Social Security Advisers' Forum and CHAR for the use of their word processors.

Obviously those people who have helped us do not necessarily agree with the views we express in the book.

The benefit rates and rules referred to in this book are those current at 1st June 1985. Taxation rates and National Insurance Contributions cited take account of announcements in the March 1985 budget.

The work for this book was undertaken by the authors in a personal capacity, and the views expressed do not represent the opinions of their employers, or of any members of the bodies responsible for their employment.

Introduction

After the Labour government's review of supplementary benefits, a group got together in Southwark to fight social security cuts. We were shaken by the experience of witnessing a Labour government putting forward proposals for cuts and by seeing the self-same proposals adopted by the Tory government which came to power in 1979. We found ourselves defending a system which was universally hated — one which stigmatized and often even humiliated claimants. As with so many anti-cuts campaign groups, we were uncomfortably on the defensive and we felt the need for the kind of positive response that socialist politics ought to be able to provide. In the absence of an already constructed satisfactory socialist approach to these questions, we decided to work within our own resources.

At the time it seemed like it ought to be a relatively easy task to develop a set of ideas about income maintenance which could readily be used in positive rather than defensive campaigning. From our own experience of the social security system, we knew broadly what was needed. Yet even the task of producing a short pamphlet proved too much for the original Southwark group. It was as if we knew what the building should look like, but we didn't know how to make it stand up — still less how to convince other people it *would* stand up. It was only when the three of us who have written this book came together around a year ago that we managed to make real progress. Even then, the writing of this book — as any of our friends will testify — has been a much more gruelling process than any of us at first anticipated.

We have not only been hampered by inexperience, but by the wider political environment. There is a convention that debates on income maintenance matters are *apolitical* and should remain so. This convention of apoliticism manifests itself on the left in a number of ways:

− in the search for a single idea which would solve income maintenance through a technical (and politically neutral) change to the structure of social security and taxation;

- in the view that everything was alright with social security until the Tory government of 1979 'broke the consensus' on income maintenance;
- in the idea that all that is needed is an injection of cash into the system — its basic structure is OK;
- in the approach which makes improvements in social security dependent on economic growth, rejecting any possibility of making major changes through the redistribution of existing resources.

The prevalence of these views on the left represents a failure to listen to the people actually affected by the issue under consideration. No one who is in regular contact with claimants and is aware of the problems they face could seriously propose these policies.

The convention of apoliticism covers the income maintenance system like a huge polythene wrapper. On the inside millions of claimants and activists kick against it, and are stifled by the lack of political oxygen; while from the outside the government prods it, attempting to manipulate the system without piercing its protective cover. Our object in this book is to tear away the packaged assumptions imposed by that wrapper. We reject the convention of apoliticism and with it the idea that social security reform should be based on sweeping technocratic solutions which claim 'political neutrality'. Indeed our starting point is that any form of income maintenance provision, and any proposal for reform, is inherently political: the task is to tease out its political implications. We therefore hope that this book will be read as a political analysis of income maintenance.

We attempt to explain how our proposals fit into a framework of socialist politics and to show how alternative approaches are incompatible with such a framework. The assumption that the social security system is inherently 'socialist' almost invariably goes unchallenged in the wider political debate and is often unquestioned within the left itself. The result is that the left gets the blame for the failings of the income maintenance system. Socialist ideas of equality and sharing become discredited among those very groups which have most to gain from socialist redistribution. Debates about income maintenance take place in a context established by the right wing. It is crucial that socialist values are reasserted in this area.

However, when debating these questions we must be careful not to fall into the trap of believing that the only task is to sort out the 'correct' set of ideas and policies. The point of developing the fundamentals of a socialist politics of income maintenance is to strengthen the campaigns for a better income maintenance system. Nor is it enough to try to persuade leaders and activists of the importance of those ideas. The left needs to take a socialist message to the people most affected — to unpaid carers, to the unemployed, to black people, to tenants in poor-quality expensive housing, to people with disabilities, to lone parents, to low-paid workers, to people with chronic illnesses and to pensioners. Moreover, in order to win the confidence of these groups and their active participation in campaigns, the left must convince them that it is serious about radical reform of the income maintenance system and that it is willing to share power with them in the process of change. We return to some of these themes when we come to look at the left's response to the government's green paper in the final chapter. For the bulk of the book our attention focuses on the principles and practicalities of socialist income maintenance policies.

Our focus in part derives from day-to-day experience of the income maintenance system. All three of us have had first-hand experience of the 'front line' between claimants and officials, where a break-down in the welfare state never seems far away. Our experience of the system and the way it treats claimants has led us to concentrate our attention on the fundamental sources of the inadequacies of contemporary income maintenance and to direct our arguments to the need for fundamental changes in the assumptions and principles on which income maintenance is based. We have therefore chosen not to put forward blueprints for social security reform. Although certain basic demands are easy to extrapolate from what we have written, we think the right place to start is with the underlying approach, not with the details of particular demands and costings.

The book begins with an examination of the present system and its disastrous effects on the lives of claimants. We also criticize proposals for reform put forward by the two main parties. In the second chapter we analyse the politics of social security by contrasting the principles which underly the present system of income maintenance with those that we advocate from a socialist perspective. In Chapters 3 to 7, we examine the key areas for an income maintenance strategy: employment and unemployment; the position of women, men and children; pensions; benefits for people with disabilities; and housing. In each chapter we criticize in detail the current provision and develop ideas for change from an understanding of how the current system affects people who rely on it — rather than from the point of view of those responsible for managing it. In Chapter 8, we discuss taxation and its relationship to benefits and examine how the overlapping of tax and benefits administration could be rationalized — not according to the dictates of administrative efficiency, but with the aim of ensuring the best possible service to the users of the income maintenance system.

We wrote the bulk of this book over the period during which Norman Fowler's 'reviews' of social security took place, and before the Government's green paper on social security was published. Doing so did not prove to be a major obstacle, since the government had made no secret of its proposals and had skilfully publicised the thinking behind them. Moreover the actual proposals for reform in the green paper bear out the analysis of Tory politics that we put forward. As much as anything else the publication of the green paper is important in that it opens up the politics of social security to wider debate. We have added a concluding chapter which examines the green paper proposals and discusses the urgent challenge they pose to socialists.

Over the last year, a succession of right-wing approaches has been put forward — most of them highly technocratic, none of them showing the slightest understanding of what life on benefits is like. These have been accompanied by a government-planned series of leaks preparing the ground for the cuts the Tories want to make. Over the same period the left has, by contrast, been almost silent, totally failing to challenge the consensus which the right has constructed around a reactionary set of principles and assumptions.

It is incredibly frustrating to see the right able to present itself as 'radical' and the left as 'conservative', while in reality there is nothing in the least radical about a Tory government scrabbling around for cuts in benefit payments. Moreover, the way they intend to make those cuts is consistent with a long-term reactionary trend in the politics of social security. But the right gets away with its radical pose, because the left has yet to develop successful oppositional politics in response to that reactionary trend.

The succession of cuts in social security has in fact started to unearth the real depth of feeling about these issues. There is widespread popular support for the idea of redistribution through social security. Many people are deeply angry at the growing inequalities between rich and poor and at the way the welfare system has been hijacked by an uncaring gang of Tory ministers. Already there are signs of people being stung into active campaigning against the right-wing assault on income maintenance. We hope this book will contribute to that process of building an oppositional politics with a future.

June 1985

1
The Starting Point

Up Until Now

In 1979 the newly elected Tory government was faced with a major problem in social security policy: the ever-accelerating increase in the number of supplementary benefit claimants. Among them were rising proportions of unemployed and single-parent claimants and, as a result, the number of children dependant on supplementary benefit (SB) showed a steady upwards trend. The government was also embarking on an economic policy intended to increase massively the already large number of unemployed people. The administration of social security was widely held to be close to break-down and the size of the social security budget (already over 25 per cent of all public spending) posed a dilemma to a government determined to cut public spending, but fearful of public disorder. On the plus side for the government, it had the *Social Assistance* report prepared for the out-going Labour government. The report made proposals for adapting the means-tested SB to a permanent 'mass role', with no extra expenditure and without the need for a radical reform of social security.

Six years on it seems they have weathered the storm in a way that could not have been predicted: the huge jump in unemployment over the last few years has been accommodated without a successful challenge to the authority of the government, electorally, industrially or on the streets. The benefits system has tottered on the verge of collapse and the fiasco of housing benefits reform has certainly damaged the government politically. But generally the signs of dissolution have tended to discredit social welfare itself rather than the government. Ministers have stood back as if to say, 'Yes, we know social security needs radical reform too. It's the foolishness of the public who want to cling on to forms of welfare provision which simply aren't adapted to the modern world — that's what gets in the way of reform.'

To the Tories 'radical reform' of course means cuts, and there were quite a few of those in the first six years of Conservative rule. Some have been pettily vindictive, such as saving £7 million by deferring the uprating of family income supplement (FIS) for up to eleven months if people make claims at the 'wrong' time of the year. Others have been very substantial, such as breaking the link between the basic retirement pension and average earnings. In total, the first six years of cuts amounted to £8 thousand million. But they didn't fundamentally alter the social security system, so its structural problems remain unresolved. In the first part of this chapter, we describe that structure and the processes by which Conservative policy has undermined and discredited it. In the second part, we look at some of the directions reform of the system could take: the type of 'radical reform' Tories would like to introduce; the far from radical approach which the Labour Party has up until now adopted; and an outline of the approach for which we argue in the rest of this book.

Criminalizing Claimants: Fraud

The notorious 'Operation Major' in Oxford typifies a new attitude to the civil rights of claimants which is having a dramatic impact on the whole benefit system. On 2 September 1982, the police and the Department of Health and Social Security (DHSS) cooperated in the mass arrest of 286 claimants. A fake benefit office was set up in a school solely for the purpose of making the arrests and anyone who entered the school was arrested. As Detective Superintendent Hedges told the pre-arranged press conference, 'We knocked off everyone who went into the building.'[1] The fraud — involving false claims from lodging houses in the city — had been known to the DHSS for some time. They had opted for the public spectacle of 'The Sting' (as the *Sun*, *Daily Star* and *Daily Express* termed it), rather than simple measures to end the fraud. Nor did they show any inclination to bring the landlords involved to book. The assumption underlying the operation was that the DHSS and the police are justified in holding claimants under suspicion — to the extent of arresting and detaining them — until they prove themselves innocent. The assumption was not challenged by the courts or by the popular media.

In fact, this assumption of guilt underlies the whole development of 'anti-fraud' work by the DHSS in recent years. The government has set up special fraud squads known as Specialist Claims Control (SCC). SCC squads circulate around local offices sifting through files randomly selected from key target groups, such as single parents and the semi-skilled unemployed. They interview, visit and/or place under observation the random sample, the main objective being to intimidate people into ending their claims rather than to detect any actual fraud. This objective is reflected in the government's statistical approach to monitoring the SCC's performance. The statistics record benefit 'saved'. If a claimant withdraws a claim after an encounter with the SCC, or their benefit is reduced, the amount of the reduction is multiplied by fifty-two and claimed as a 'saving' by the SCC; this is done irrespective of whether the cause of the saving has anything to do with fraud. This kind of procedure has nothing to do with fraud as such; it is in fact a DHSS-organized counter take-up campaign.

The tactics used in the SCC anti-take-up work are no longer restricted to means-tested benefits. The Department of Employment has set up Regional Benefit Investigation Teams in imitation of the SCC's. The letter sent to staff in the department advertising jobs in these teams made the philosophy crystal clear:

> The techniques require not so much the dogged pursuit of evidence looked for in normal fraud work but a lightness of touch in being able to confront claimants with a few suspicious facts which will lead the suspect either to declare work or otherwise leave the register.
> This quality is more important than benefit experience and it requires that staff recruited should have an ability to think quickly on their feet when interviewing claimants suspected of fraud.[2]

These developments have as yet been largely confined to specialist squads and initiatives. But it is easy to see — especially in the context of the effectiveness of joint union and claimant campaigns against the roving squads — that the next development is likely to be the integration of the 'anti-take-up' method into regular fraud work, with random file checks, interviews, surveillance and so on. Indeed, the trend is already observable. In the Woolwich area, for example, fraud officers now interview *every* claimant who reports a lost giro payment for suspected fraud. Simply declaring a need has become grounds for suspicion of dishonesty.

The main causes of fraud are the abysmally low levels of benefits and the rules of entitlement which ensure that it is very difficult for claimants to do many things which appear perfectly legitimate *without* committing fraud. Take the example of someone who is long-term unemployed. She doesn't even get the slightly higher rate of benefit paid to other long-term claimants (such as single parents and the disabled). So she decides to try and supplement her income with a part-time job. She finds that she loses all her earnings after the first £4 and that she is required to make a weekly return to the DHSS. This will almost invariably cause her benefit to be paid late. Finally, if she perseveres and hangs on to her job for a few months, the Department of Employment will probably decide that she is permanently employed as a part-time worker and her benefit will be cut off altogether, even if her part-time earnings are well below SB level.

Criminalizing Claimants: Internal Controls

'Entitlement to Supplementary Benefit of persons who have arrived here and do not have a permanent right of abode in the UK depends on the status granted to them by the Home Office on entry.'[3]

This statement in the DHSS 'S' Manual giving guidance to its benefits staff introduces an implicit threat to black people attempting to claim SB. Any tests of immigration status which form part of benefit assessments inevitably discriminate against black residents in Britain.[4] Benefits staff will consider that black claimants are more likely to have insecure or illegal immigration status than white claimants.

In 1980 a new statutory requirement was introduced into the SB scheme: that benefit officers must take account of immigration status in the assessment of claims. As a result of the changes, the needs of claimants are ignored for SB purposes if they are subject to a Home Office requirement that they should not have 'recourse to public funds'. This new rule affects, for example, students, fiancés and fiancées, and the dependants of work-permit holders. The more general rules concerning couples and maintenance have also come to be used specifically against black claimants. In 1982 it was ruled that an Asian woman was dependant on her husband, even though he had never entered this country.[5] Women whose husbands have returned to the Asian sub-continent for prolonged visits have been told that if they claim SB their husbands will be prosecuted — for failing to maintain them.

These types of tests are spreading steadily through other parts of the benefit system also. The requirement not to have recourse to public funds is a general threat hanging over the claiming of all benefits — because the Home Office refuses to state which benefits immigrants can claim without infringing the requirement. In September 1984 an immigration status test was introduced into the housing benefit (HB) scheme for the first time. A range of residence conditions discriminate against black people, who are more likely than whites to fail them.

For black claimants, contact with the DHSS frequently involves passport checks or demands for other immigration documents. The process of claiming SB, and to a lesser degree other benefits, appears to the black claimant to imply an automatic suspicion that s/he may be an illegal immigrant. The unit at DHSS headquarters which deals with immigration matters is known to have free and open liaison with the Home Office over individual cases. Indeed the form on which staff are supposed to report immigration cases to the unit is addressed to the Home Office as well.[6] There is therefore no confidentiality whatsoever attaching to SB claims. Claimants must subject themselves to a sophisticated system of internal immigration control administered jointly by the DHSS and the Home Office.

Social Security is a key element in the growing system known as 'internal controls'. As the external immigration controls imposed in the 1960s and 1970s have become less relevant to the control of the permanent black population within Great Britain, so the government has moved to impose controls on that population internally. Fleet Street has actively promoted the application of these controls to the social security system with headlines such as 'Foreigners Given Free Holidays — Another Big Exclusive — The Softest Touch in Europe'.[7]

The changes which have taken place with regard to black claimants over the last few years are not only indicative of the general moves towards 'internal controls'. They also form part of the process of criminalizing the act of claiming benefits. The DHSS has stopped defining itself as a 'soft' agency allied to the personal social services and has instead drawn closer to the agencies of law enforcement — the Home Office and the police.

The New Look DHSS

It came as little surprise when the new Conservative government moved swiftly to implement reforms along the lines of the *Social Assistance* report which had been drawn up for the out-going Labour government. Ministers had predetermined the main lines of its conclusions by ordering that it should not recommend any additional expenditure on social security and that it should not consider the relationship between SB and non-means-tested benefits. Inevitably therefore the report simply considered various options for adapting the means-tested SB to the 'mass role' which had already been thrust upon it and which the Labour government wished to retain for it. The main feature of the new scheme which took effect from November 1980 was a new legal framework which eliminated most areas of discretion. The reforms brought SB and National Insurance benefits under a uniform legal structure, and the way was cleared for the unification of the two systems of decision-making in 1984. This was a significant step in undermining the traditional distinctions between the means-tested SB and the insurance system. Insurance benefits rely on a contribution test, are not means-tested and are therefore commonly seen as 'respectable', whereas SB is a benefit for people on very low incomes and is means-tested.

The new scheme caused widespread outrage among claimants. It soon became clear that when the government talked about 'simplification' they were referring to an administrative idea — nothing to do with how readily the scheme could be understood by claimants. A complete set of the relevant regulations currently costs around £50. The government attempted to repeat the pattern with the introduction of the HB scheme in 1982/3. Again, the changes left the basic structure of housing benefits untouched, but responsibility for administering the resulting mess was shifted from the DHSS to local councils. The most significant permanent effect of the reforms is likely to have been to undermine still further the distinction between means-tested benefits and National Insurance. Take the example of pensioners. Prior to 1982 many pensioners would claim rent and rate rebates in preference to SB, even if they would have been better off on SB. A distinction was clearly perceived between getting the contributory state retirement pension, plus rent and rate rebates, and getting SB. This may have been undesirable and was certainly irrational, because rent and rate rebates were themselves means-tested, but the distinction existed. It took HB to blow it away, by lumping together all pensioners who need any form of assistance with housing costs. The standard of administration and treatment of claimants has fallen to the level previously provided by the DHSS, often even lower, but now it affects far more people. A large number of people feel themselves dragged into an increasingly all-pervasive system of means-testing.

Blurring the distinction between means-tested and non-means-tested benefits fits in with what appears to have been the Tory approach to social security in the first six years of office. Despite the important cuts referred to above, in this period they did not attempt any fundamental restructuring of social security. They pursued a strategy of 'active erosion', allowing the twin pressures of mass unemployment and staff cuts to bring the system to the brink of collapse. Where the system broke down temporarily or locally the government was able to observe the effects at a safe political distance and at the same time point to the need for a radical 're-think' of social welfare.[8]

The government's approach was evident in its handling of the strike at the Newcastle computer centre in 1984. The strike started in response to a government move to cut pay by around £50,000 a year by changing the shift allowance system. Despite the small amount of savings, the government was willing to pay between £80 million (government estimate) and £150 million (union estimate) to defeat the strike.[9] In the seven months of the strike, the whole of the social security system was thrown into chaos. The strike meant that all new claims for contributory benefits had to be assessed and paid manually. Staff in local offices were transferred to undertake the November uprating of benefits and to write giros. Visits to deal with claims for grants or weekly additions to SB were postponed or simply suspended. Delays lengthened and queuing at post offices to cash pensions and child benefit orders under emergency arrangements frequently took more than an hour. But the government succeeded in imposing a defeat on the unions which was important to its long-term strategy of major staff cuts. At the same time the credibility of the benefits system was further eroded and the government could take comfort from the fact that the public had accepted such major disruption to the system without major protests occurring.

To date staff 'cuts' have taken the form of worsening the ratio between staff and claimants. Whereas in 1979 each member of staff working on SB claims dealt with around a hundred claimants, by 1984 s/he had to deal with 132 — and a much higher proportion of those claimants were unemployed or single parents, generating a far greater workload than pensioner claimants. The government's hope is that computerization will reduce the number of staff needed in the DHSS by up to a quarter, from 100,000 to between 75,000 and 80,000.[10] The DHSS currently uses 8,000 different forms *internally* and another 12,000 externally. The savings of computerization will apply to mass administrative tasks such as producing order books.

Despite the glossy hi-tech image summoned to mind by the idea of computerization, the introduction of new technology complements the process of criminalizing claimants which we discussed in the previous two sections. Postal claim forms (as opposed to interviews or visits to each new claimant), staff cuts and computerization all entail less personal contact between benefit officials and claimants. In turn, the reduction of personal contact justifies an increase of random fraud checks of the sort carried out by the Specialist Claims Control squads. For example, in May 1984 a confidential DHSS paper recommended that all benefit claims should be made by post and that all visits to check and advise on benefit entitlement should end.[11] The staff thereby released should be transferred to carry out random fraud checks on the same claimants they would previously have advised and assisted. Postal claiming has now been extended from the unemployed to all claimants, though still at the moment on a voluntary basis. The prospect of a benefits system in which assessments are undertaken by computers while the main function of staff is to 'control' claims is a nightmare which can be averted, but only if it is taken seriously.

Now

The Structure of Benefits

The social security system introduced shortly after the war was based primarily on the 'binary principle' of benefits, and the principle still lies at the heart of the current benefit structure. The principle applies to two categories of benefits. There are National Insurance (NI) benefits, such as unemployment benefit, retirement pension, maternity allowance and invalidity benefit. These NI benefits are paid according to contributions paid by the claimant (so they are called 'contributory' benefits). Claimants can also sometimes be 'credited' with contributions if they are unable to pay them, for example, if they are unemployed. NI benefits are not means-tested: were the Governor of the Bank of England to be sacked, he could claim and receive £28.45 a week Unemployment Benefit so long as he had sufficient NI contributions. It would be irrelevant whether or not he possessed any wealth.

The other category to which the binary principle applies is that of means-tested benefits. These are the ones the Governor of the Bank of England would be unlikely to qualify for, even if he were to be given the push. These include supplementary benefit (including both the allowance for non-pensioners and supplementary pension); housing benefit; family income supplement; educational welfare benefits and around forty other types of benefit. The characteristic of these benefits is that entitlement and the precise level of each benefit depends on the income and sometimes the savings of the claimant. The income taken into account will normally include any NI benefits which the claimant receives and any income received by the rest of the claimant's family. For example, a woman who is pregnant and getting maternity pay from her employer and maternity allowance (an NI benefit) may wish to claim help with her housing costs. If she claims HB, both sources of income (the pay and the allowance) will be taken into account and will act to reduce the level of her HB.

It is crucial to the binary principle of benefit assessment that NI and means-tested benefits are not *exclusive* alternatives. You can be entitled to neither, to either one, or to both. This is represented in Table 1.1.

Table 1.1
THE BINARY PRINCIPLE OF BENEFIT ASSESSMENT

	NI Benefit	*Means-tested Benefits*
(1) You're not entitled to any benefit	No	No
(2) You're only entitled to NI benefits	Yes	No
(3) You're entitled to both types of benefit	Yes	Yes
(4) You're only entitled to means-tested benefits	No	Yes

Take the example of a married woman. She's working and so is her husband. Initially she may be entitled to no benefits at all, as in (1) in Table 1.1. She is then made redundant and she claims unemployment benefit, which she gets because of her contributions while in work; but she can't claim means-tested SB, because her husband's earnings are too high, so she is in category (2). At this point she separates from her husband and, without his income to rely on, she becomes eligible for SB in addition to her unemployment benefit, as in (3). Finally, a year after she is made redundant, her unemployment benefit ends and she becomes solely reliant on SB and other means-tested benefits, as in (4).

This binary principle seems to work symmetrically and almost logically. But there is also a tension in the relationship which is illustrated in the example when the woman loses her unemployment benefit and becomes solely reliant on means-tested benefits. At this point she doesn't actually lose any money, because the level of her SB increases 'pound for pound' to compensate for the loss of unemployment benefit. The implication of this is that there is no practical difference for her between stages (3) and (4). Whether or not she gets an NI benefit becomes irrelevant once she has to claim SB. The binary principle seems to establish a category of means-tested benefits to *complement* the contributory ones, but in fact the new category partially invalidates the principles of those contributory benefits. Once you need the means-tested benefits to 'top up' your insurance benefits, your contributions become worthless in practice. The steady reduction in the real value of NI benefits has made this problem more common.

Apart from being essentially flawed in this way, the binary principle is by no means applied uniformly throughout the benefit system. Many benefits fall outside the two categories which it imposes. Firstly, there are a range of state benefits which do not depend on contributions, but which behave in much the same way as NI benefits: they can be topped up by means-tested benefits and they act to reduce the level of those benefits because they are taken into account as 'income'. The most important of these is child benefit, but there are also industrial injury benefits, severe disablement allowance (for the severely disabled) and invalid care allowance (for some people providing care in the home).[12] The second type are also non-contributory, but they don't behave like NI benefits at all; they are almost completely outside the 'binary principle', because they are usually ignored when the major means-tested benefits are assessed. The main examples are mobility allowance (for people with severe difficulty in walking) and attendance allowance (for severely disabled people who need care in the home). Both of these benefits can normally be claimed on top of SB or HB without affecting their level.[13]

Insurance and non-contributory benefits are often referred to as 'contingent' benefits because one of their features is that they are paid as a result of a particular external event, for example, sickness. Grouping these benefits together in this way tends to obscure the important differences between contributory and non-contributory benefits. It also blurs the distinction between benefits paid to people because they don't have a wage, such as unemployment and sickness benefits, and benefits which are related to extra costs, such as attendance allowance.

Finally, benefits provided privately under state regulation are becoming increasingly important as a result of the Tory objectives of reducing public expenditure on social security and increasing reliance on the market. The degree of state regulation varies considerably. Statutory sick pay operates very much like a benefit paid on behalf of the state by employers, whereas occupational pensions are at the other extreme with minimal state regulation. In terms of their interaction with other benefits, private benefits and pensions

are treated very much like NI benefits: they are treated as income and therefore
reduce the beneficiary's entitlement to means-tested benefits. The big practical
difference is that they are far more likely to eliminate the need for means-tested
benefits altogether, by giving the beneficiary an adequate income. They create a
theoretical possibility which clearly attracts the Tory policy-makers: to create a
system based on two stark alternatives — private welfare or the means test.

Key Facts about Social Security

The current level of expenditure on social security is often described as being
'out of control', or more moderately as in obvious need of 'trimming'. In

Table 1.2
SOCIAL SECURITY EXPENDITURE, 1984/5

Benefit	Expenditure (£ thousand million)	% of Social Security Expenditure	No. of Recipients (million)
Non-means-tested benefits			
Retirement pensions	15.435	40.21	9.260
Invalidity benefit	1.928	5.02	0.740
Unemployment benefit	1.538	4.01	0.970
Attendance, invalid care and mobility allowances	0.938	2.44	0.850
Child benefit	4.291	11.18	12.455
One-parent benefit	0.122	0.32	0.570
Means-tested benefits			
Supplementary pensions	0.792	2.06	1.520
Supplementary allowances	5.365	13.97	2.790
Family income supplement	0.131	0.34	0.205
Housing benefit—rent rebates and allowances	2.461	6.41	4.105
Administration and services	1.600	4.17	

Source: Extrapolation from Central Statistical Office, *Social Trends 15*, London 1985.

1984/5 the total expenditure on social security was £38,391 million. This made up nearly 30 per cent of all public expenditure. But the importance of the sheer size of this budget should not be exaggerated. In 1983 it only accounted for 14 per cent of all household income, only slightly ahead of income from private pensions, annuities and returns on savings and investments, which totalled 13 per cent. Meanwhile, 62 per cent of household income came from wages and salaries.[14] Moreover, as discussed in Chapter 8, the way in which the size of the social security budget is presented is in itself misleading.

Of the £38.4 thousand million spent in 1984/5, very nearly half (49 per cent) went on contributory pensions of one sort or another, and child benefits took a further tenth (11 per cent). By contrast, the main object of media criticism, SB payments to non-pensioners, accounted for only one-seventh of social security expenditure. Table 1.2 gives a breakdown of social security expenditure in that year on some of the major benefits. It also shows how many people got each benefit.

Despite the relatively low level of expenditure on SB, the scheme is of central importance. Because of the way in which the binary principle operates, if a claimant only receives an SB payment of one or two pounds per week her/his standard of living is depressed to the same subsistence level as another claimant whose only income is SB. This is of especial significance in light of the fact that two-thirds of all SB claimants have been on SB for more than a year.[15] Moreover, since SB is assessed on the basis of the family unit, the true number of people living at this poverty level far exceeds the actual number of recipients shown in the table above. It is therefore important to look at who lives on SB and how the numbers have grown since 1979 (see Table 1.3)

Table 1.3
WHO LIVES ON SUPPLEMENTARY BENEFIT?

	1982	1979
Pensioners	1,780,000	1,720,000
Unemployed	1,722,000	566,000
Single parents	415,000	306,000
Sick and disabled	240,000	210,000
Widows under sixty	20,000	19,000
Adult dependants	1,080,000	593,000
Children	1,721,000	923,000
Others	90,000	32,000
Total	7,068,000	4,369,000

Source: DHSS, *Social Security Statistics 1984*, London 1984

To understand the social security budget and statistics about the number of claimants, we must become accustomed to dealing with large numbers: claimants, on the other hand, must get used to dealing with very small numbers. The ordinary rate of SB for a single person is just £28.05, and for a couple it is £45.55; all pensioners and those claimants *other than the unemployed* who are on SB for more than a year get £35.70 (single) or £57.10 (couple). For each child aged ten or under, you get just £9.60 — and don't forget child benefit is deducted from that amount. These amounts are supposed to include all usual living expenses including fuel, food and clothing (but not housing costs). The NI benefit rates are barely more generous. A single person on unemployment benefit gets £28.45, and a couple on retirement pension receives £57.30. Indeed the lack of a significant differential between insurance benefits and SB is a major underlying cause of the fact that so many people have to claim means-tested benefits. A pensioner whose only income is basic-rate retirement pension is bound to have to claim either SB or HB in order to meet his/her housing costs.

As a result of the way benefits interact, taking into account the generally low rate of benefit, huge numbers of people are forced to live on or below the poverty line. Despite Norman Fowler's attempt to discredit measures of poverty based on the SB level, it is clear that those forced to live at or near this level will experience serious material deprivation. Yet even in 1981, before mass unemployment had really started to escalate rapidly, 13.59 million people had incomes equal to less than 140 per cent of the SB scale rate.[16]

Throughout the social security system, hundreds of millions of pounds go unclaimed. The DHSS estimated that in 1981 only 71 per cent of those eligible for SB actually claimed it.[17] Moreover those who do claim the benefits they are entitled to appear generally dissatisfied with the service they receive from the DHSS. In Greenwich at the end of 1983, two out of every five claimants expressed themselves dissatisfied with the service from the local DHSS offices.[18] Social security is a mass scheme in Britain involving large numbers of people and huge sums of money, but it fails to deliver adequate benefits in a humane fashion to those who need them.

From Now On

Until recently, two positions seemed to define the whole field of debate on social security. One position favoured the extension and reinforcement of the insurance principle; the other supported the greater use of means tests. But there was a crucial twist to the argument put by the pro-insurance lobby. Believing that it was unreasonable or impractical to raise flat-rate benefits to a level above that of means-tested benefits, it was suggested that you could achieve at least some success by introducing earnings-related NI benefits. At least then some people (the better paid) would no longer have to rely on means tests.

Thus the two lobbies for the two opposing elements of the binary categorization came to have something in common: both favoured forms of selectivity; and, in the event, the two forms of selectivity were to prove remarkably compatible. Both forms of selectivity reflect the widely held view that social security is a drain on national resources and that therefore benefit expenditure must be tightly contained. The proponents of earnings-related benefits put forward other schemes — such as state earnings-related pensions and earnings-related supplements to short-term NI benefits. These selected higher income earners for favourable treatment, giving them benefits high enough to lift them above the level of means-tested benefits as a trade-off for paying higher contributions. Meanwhile those who favoured means-testing put forward benefits such as FIS and rent rebates to 'target' those low income groups who would in any case qualify for little or no earnings-related benefit. So, although apparently based on opposing philosophies, the two approaches complemented each other neatly in practice and in fact elements of both have been acceped by all post-war governments.

The New Tory Approach

The Thatcher government has been credited with breaking the post-war consensus on many issues, and income maintenance is no exception. The best way of understanding the Thatcher approach is to see the way in which its logic has evolved over time. The starting point has been a rejection of the cosy partnership between the two forms of selectivity discussed above. This rejection has been based on two closely linked principles: firstly, that state expenditure should be reduced as far as possible; secondly, that the state should not intervene (either through the benefits system or through economic policy) to protect people from poverty. The consequence of these principles is the view that the state benefits system should confine itself to maintaining those in poverty at a subsistence level through means-testing. It should not get involved in non-means-tested benefits such as child benefit or earnings-related pensions: those who wish to avoid poverty should rely on the market, that is, wages and private pensions.

However, this view involves a paradox, which we will examine in greater detail in Chapter 3. One of the rationales of the Thatcherite approach is the reinforcement of incentives. The rejection of NI and earnings-related benefits achieves this in one way — by widening the chasm between those who can survive respectably in the market-place and those compelled to resort to means tests. But in another way it undermines incentives, again because of the flaw identified in the binary principle earlier; only this time it is the relationship between wages and means-tested benefits which produces the problem. Once someone is forced to claim means-tested benefits it matters much less to them in cash terms whether they work or not and, if they do work, how much they earn. As they earn more, their benefits decrease and their net income is more or less stagnant — the very antithesis to Thatcher's enterprise culture!

If the commitment to means-testing is sacrosanct, there are broadly two solutions to this problem. Means-tested benefits can be withdrawn more slowly, so that people can earn more and still get some help, and earning more becomes correspondingly more worthwhile. But this approach conflicts with the first Tory objective — cutting public expenditure. Therefore Tory policy has done the reverse (especially as far as housing benefits are concerned) and lowered the maximum level at which benefits are payable. So if cutting social security expenditure is sacrosanct, there is only one direction possible: the minimum subsistence income level guaranteed by means-tested benefits must be lowered. By starting from a lower floor, it is possible to have some incentives and a relatively low cut-off point at which benefits cease to be payable altogether.

It is fairly clear what directions Tory policy would now like to take. Prior to publishing his Green Paper, Norman Fowler has made it clear that he would like to get rid of the state earnings-related pension; that he wants to make social security more selective and therefore cut back on non-means-tested benefits, for example, by freezing child benefit; and that the poverty line needs to be re-defined, which means lowering the income level guaranteed by the state. So Norman Fowler is proposing a series of major cuts. These would make individual means tests, for example, in the HB and SB schemes, much harsher. He is doing so under the cover of a major review of the structure of social security, which he claims is comparable to the Beveridge Report. In general, the developments over the first six years of Tory rule have paved the way for a system revolving around a more 'rational' unified means test and the eventual abolition of NI and other non-means-tested benefits. But it is much less clear how far down this road the Tories can go, or even wish to go. Although a unified means test of this sort seems to be a rational way of implementing the Tories' policy of increasing selectivity, it would have the significant disadvantage of making explicit the underlying structure of means tests. It would then be easier for people to understand how unfair that basic structure is. It would also intensify the political difficulties of levying high NI contributions after the benefits derived from those contributions have been fundamentally undermined.

Back to Beveridge

Depressingly, the main current alternative to the new Tory vision of income maintenance is an essentially backward-looking one. This is the view that we should go back to the principles, if not all the details, of the Beveridge Report, the report which preceded the post-war Labour government's major reforms of the system. This view is still generally held within the Labour Party and the trade union movement. It was this report which — perhaps unwittingly — placed the binary principle at the heart of British income maintenance. We have already made it clear that such a principle has fundamental drawbacks, in that the presence of the means test undermines the insurance principle and indeed tends to pollute the whole system. But the proponents of this strategy would no doubt argue that they propose making insurance benefits so comprehensive and generous that the means tests would become redundant.

The phrase 'back to Beveridge' trips off the tongue so easily that it is easy to use it without thinking what it actually means. We think that it may be worthwhile to point out the weaknesses of the original Beveridge Report, even judged on the simple standard of its strategy for the abolition of poverty:

(1) *People without Contributions.* Since it was a contributory insurance plan, the Beveridge Report has no answer to the needs of those who haven't worked and who haven't contributed. These include those incapacitated from an early age by a disability and unemployed school leavers.

(2) *Housing Costs.* Beveridge has no answer to the problem of variations in rent levels. Without such an answer, the enhanced role of means-testing is more or less assured, because no government is likely to be willing to raise insurance benefits to a level high enough to meet the highest rents.

(3) *Single Parents.* Beveridge assumed the universality of the nuclear family with the husband and wife 'working as a team' — the wife at home and the husband in employment. His plan does not include a benefit, insurance or otherwise, for single parents.

(4) *Low Pay and the Family Wage.* Beveridge didn't have an answer to the problem of low pay. He assumed that a system of 'children's allowances' would be instituted which would mitigate the problem. But he himself argued that these should only be offering 'help' to parents and, for this reason, the needs of the first child would be ignored. Moreover he assumed that married women would be full-time housewives and mothers, supported by their husbands' wages. Thus the hopes of abolishing poverty rest on a 'family wage' sufficient to cover the needs of the wage-earner, his dependant wife and one child. But apart from the unacceptability and increasing inaccuracy of such an assumption about the role of women, Beveridge has no methods for ensuring that wages do not fall below this 'family minimum', or that when achieved it is distributed fairly within the family.

Michael Meacher, as shadow spokesperson on social services, has been attempting to initiate a debate around these issues. At the time of writing, his book has not been published, so it is not possible to make detailed comments; however, his approach appears not to make a fundamental break with the 'back to Beveridge' approach. His public statements have been ambiguous over the extent to which he thinks the Labour Party should move away from its traditional support for contributory, earnings-related and family-based benefits. He favours a substantial reduction in means-testing, but he has not made proposals to eliminate it altogether. Despite the shortcomings of these ideas, the attempt to promote discussion is long overdue. To date, the Labour Party's response has been profoundly depressing. The major objective of national figures on both the left and right of the party seems to be to avoid or even stifle debate on issues of principle. There seems to be an overwhelming fear of the controversy which could result from a political examination of income maintenance.

Tackling the Real Problem

In this book we put forward an approach radically different to the two options we have considered here: extending and rationalizing the means test, or returning to the principles of Beveridge. We are not going to put forward the arguments for our approach at this point, but simply explain the general framework.

We favour two categories of benefits to replace the whole of the present benefit system. The first category is that of 'positional benefits' paid to the various groups of people who are not in full-time work and so cannot rely on a wage as an adequate source of income. We call these 'positional benefits' because they relate to an individual's 'position' when s/he claims benefit — as an unemployed person, a carer, someone who is sick, a part-time worker, etc. The second category is that of 'cost-related benefits', for those people who have a need to incur extra expenditure, whether in work or not, for example, those with high housing costs. This approach would avoid the use of means tests and make contributions tests unnecessary. Moreover, it would relate benefit payments directly to the social causes of need. Thus, for example, the unemployed, the sick, the elderly and those engaged in child-care (whether as single parents or in couples) would receive a flat-rate postional benefit, irrespective of income or contributions. Disabled people would receive a cost-related benefit to help with mobility, care and other needs. Despite its universalist character, such a system could be made to be strongly progressive through a comprehensive taxation system. In order to overcome the current obstacles to part-time work, we propose that it should be possible to claim benefit as unemployed on a part-time basis.

The principle of relating benefits to needs would be extended to those in full-time work, in that they should be able to receive benefits for additional needs on the same basis as those people not working. As at present, parents would be able to claim child benefit when working, but the level should be increased substantially to approach the full costs of supporting a child. Similarly, disabled people would be able to receive additional benefits whether or not they are working. We do not, however, believe that the benefit system should meet the basic needs of those in full-time work, by some form of 'social credit', as has been proposed, for example, by the National Federation of Claimants' Unions. Such needs would be the responsibility of employers to meet through the wages system, and that responsibility would be enforceable through a minimum wage. Nevertheless we recognize that in the medium term it is impossible for wages or a flat-rate benefit to cover the wide variation in housing costs which presently exists: we therefore propose a taxable housing allowance which would vary according to the level of housing costs. Benefits, taxation and entitlement to minimum wages should all be assessed on an individual basis. Living relationships should be a matter of choice. At the moment they are not: many women suffer an enforced financial dependency on men, because of the use of the family unit as the basis of income maintenance assessment and because of the obstacles to women (especially mothers) obtaining genuine financial independence through work. All adults should be given financial independence with dignity. We also propose a uniform system which would not discriminate on grounds of sex, race or locality. In turn, that entails guaranteeing the confidentiality of treatment under the income maintenance system, particularly in order to safeguard the rights of black claimants.

In the next chapter we discuss the principles which have led us to adopt these proposals, and in the following chapters we examine in more detail the shortcomings of the present system and the advantages of our approach.

Notes

1. Ros Franey, *Poor Law*, Char. London 1983.
2. *Guardian*, 9 August 1983.
3. DHSS, 'S' Manual, London 1984, para. 3951.
4. Hugo Storey, 'UK Immigration Controls and the Welfare State', *Journal of Social Welfare Law*, January 1984.
5. Social Security Commissioner's Decision, R(SB) 12/82, HMSO.
6. DHSS, 'S' Manual, appendix 2 — draft letters, 'DLSB/A 11'.
7. *Daily Mail*, 21 August 1984.
8. See Sally Coetze, 'Flat Broke' — How the Welfare State Collapsed in Birmingham, Birmingham 1983.
9. *Financial Times*, 18 December 1984.
10. DHSS *Social Security Operational Strategy: A Framework for the Future*, London 1982.
11. *Guardian*, 10 May 1984.
12. Benefits for the disabled are described in greater detail in Chapter 6.

13. The government has recently introduced regulations undermining this advantage of attendance allowance by taking it into account in the assessment of supplementary benefit for people living in residential care and nursing homes.

14. All figures from Central Statistical Office, *Social Trends 15*, London 1985.

15. All figures from DHSS, *Social Security Statistics 1984*, London 1985.

16. *Social Trends 15*.

17. *Social Security Statistics 1984*.

18. Greenwich Welfare Rights Unit, *Breadline Greenwich: Welfare Rights Implications*, London 1985.

2
Key Concepts and Basic Principles

The habit has grown up of looking back nostalgically on the years of the post-war Labour government as the era of socialist achievement and victory. In particular the achievement of establishing the welfare state is cited. During the nineteenth and early twentieth centuries, a definable group of unwaged individuals was gradually constructed for the first time. Increased life expectancy implied that retirement (even if involuntary), rather than death, might end working life. Children and women were increasingly excluded from paid employment outside the home. The work-force was progressively de-casualized, creating a pool of unemployed, rather than simply under-employed, individuals. The social welfare measures which were slowly introduced in response to this new situation, culminating in the post-war creation of the 'welfare state', were rarely the goals of socialist agitation, though often they were introduced in response to actual or feared popular unrest. The labour movement was fairly clear in its rejection of the solutions offered by private charity and the Poor Law, but tended to turn instead to the solutions of 'self-help' (in the form of friendly societies and union benefits) and family responsibility (arguing for the 'family wage'). Indeed, repugnance at the workings of the Poor Law, with the humiliations of the workhouse and means test, clearly led to positions of mistrust and hostility to state-organized welfare.

The post-war social security system undoubtedly reflected a popular demand for assurance that the fruits of war would not be a repeat of the 'peace' of the 1920s and 1930s. But socialist thought had little to contribute in the formulation of demands concerning the social welfare system. Historically the socialist movement has not had a firm position on social welfare issues, enabling it to challenge the solutions which have been put forward by pro-capitalist political forces. Yet so great has been the confusion surrounding income maintenance issues that the right has been able to identify 'state spending on welfare' with socialism itself. The way in which solutions to income maintenance issues have

have been selected for their compatibility with a capitalist economic and social system has been disguised. The aim of this chapter is, first of all, to identify the principles lying behind those solutions. We then review some of the theoretical questions of relevance to a socialist approach. Finally, we attempt to define a socialist position on the principles of income maintenance.

Right-wing Answers to Left-wing Questions

The need for societies to have income maintenance systems raises questions which socialist thought should be particularly capable of resolving. At least in theory, income maintenance depends on values of sharing and cooperation: the idea that society should support all its members and ensure their welfare at a reasonable level, irrespective of their ability to earn money, has an implicit socialist content. Yet in the past these questions have generally been given right wing answers. To see why let us start by asking what income maintenance is: we can then discuss the particular principles which have underpinned British income maintenance.

Systems of income maintenance are systems of direct social intervention in the allocation of costs and incomes to individuals. In this book we discuss income maintenance in relation to the incomes of individuals, because this is how the state actually pays benefits and deducts taxes — to and from individuals.[1] Moreover, it is important to examine the actual effect of income maintenance on individuals, rather than looking at the position of families as a whole. There are three main ways in which income maintenance operates. The state can redistribute incomes from one group of individuals to another through taxation and benefits; or it can intervene to guarantee minimum incomes for particular groups, for example, by setting a minimum wage for workers; or it can intervene to reduce the cost of necessary items, for example, by using rent controls to ensure that housing can be afforded.

In order to be properly considered as part of the income maintenance system, measures must have specific effects on people whose incomes are inadequate to meet their needs. The measures must either raise their incomes or reduce their costs, so that overall their spending power is more closely matched to their needs. However, income maintenance measures invariably have other effects in addition to financially assisting people with low incomes. Firstly, income maintenance payments transfer spending from the better off through taxation — so they lose financially. Secondly, the rules and conditions of benefits shape the lives of claimants, often adversely, as well as giving them an entitlement to money. Income maintenance therefore almost always involved losses for individuals as well as gains: the single parent who cannot enter into friendships with men for fear of losing her only source of income; the higher income earner who pays taxes which go towards pensions; the unemployed person who cannot legally work part-time without losing benefit; the employer who is forced to pay higher wages by statutory minimum wage rates; and so on. At the heart of the process of evaluating income maintenance politically are these difficult questions. Who really does benefit? And who ought to benefit?

The widespread existence of systems of income maintenance within capitalist societies implies the failure of the market to achieve, unaided, the satisfaction of needs. The market has proved unable to feed children, to house people, to care for the disabled, to pay adequate pensions, and so on. This is a major reason why the right dislikes social welfare so much. It is not just that it costs private companies and individuals money — after all, so do defence and the police force. The difference is that the right has never claimed that market forces are able to maintain law and order without the aid of the state. But it *does* claim that capitalism is able to meet needs. The necessity for income maintenance is a daily reminder that capitalism doesn't work.

The failure of the market in this respect can best be understood in terms of the major historical development we outlined above: the construction and continued existence of a large group of unwaged individuals. The make-up of this group has varied substantially over the last century, but at present it can be seen to include children, students, adults undertaking child-care, sick and disabled people, the unemployed, the elderly, those caring for disabled or elderly people, and those who choose not to take paid employment such as some married women. There are in fact some 'market-oriented' solutions to the problem of wagelessness. These solutions are theoretically consistent with the idea of an economy based wholly on the market system. They can be grouped in the following way:

(1) Personal savings (for example, for retirement), and insurance (for example, against sickness).
(2) Family dependancy and responsibility (for example, for children, disabled people and the elderly).
(3) Charity.
(4) Occupational welfare (for example, an employer-run pension fund).
(5) Compensation (for example, for accidents at work).

However these solutions could never make more than a very limited contribution to meeting the needs of those without wages. For example, workers are not paid enough to enable them to save enough for retirement, or to fully support dependants. Charity is a voluntary re-distribution of income and as such could only ever be marginal in its effects.

Given the necessity for some kind of income maintenance, because of the inadequacy of the market, it is possible to identify a strategy for income maintenance which can be termed 'pro-capitalist'. Such a strategy has both a negative and a positive aspect. Negatively, it proposes a form of state intervention which disturbs as little as possible the operation of the market — for example, by trying to avoid undermining the financial imperative to work and by allowing the maximum scope for the 'market solutions' listed above to operate. Positively, it seeks to model state provision on the market solutions and to reflect market values in the operation of the state system.

An example of the negative element of the 'pro-capitalist' strategy can be seen in the contemporary politics of income maintenance. As we discussed in the last chapter, a major thrust of Tory policy is to reduce the role of the state in income maintenance: to force those with incomes above a rock-bottom poverty line to rely on private, that is, market solutions. The 'positive' element is reflected in the current system of state benefits. This structure has been closely modelled on the same market solutions:

(1) *Personal Savings and Insurance.* As we showed in Chapter 1, the insurance principle has been central to the development of the post-war social security system.

(2) *Family Dependancy and Responsibility.* This principle runs through almost every aspect of the income maintenance system, with the use of the family unit as the basis for benefit assessment and taxation. (See Chapter 4 for a fuller discussion of these issues.)

(3) *Charity.* The principle of charity is mirrored in the (ever-increasing) use of means tests. They both operate according to the same principles of selectivity. The distinctive feature of both means tests and charity is that the state intervenes after the operation of the market to 'rescue' the individual casualties of the market system — those for whom neither wages nor 'self-help' has provided a subsistence level of income.

(4) *Occupational Welfare.* Occupational welfare is the provision of welfare at the workplace or by the employer. Examples are the provision of perks and fringe benefits such as company cars, or of essential services such as nurseries. The Conservative government is placing an increasing emphasis on occupational welfare, particularly employer-run pension schemes. The role of the state becomes one of encouraging occupational welfare and regulating it to ensure that it is an adequate substitute for state benefits.

(5) *Compensation.* The principle of compensation can be seen at work most explicitly in benefits for the disabled. These benefits are not primarily based on the degree of disability and needs of the person, but instead are closely linked to the *cause* of disability.

Income maintenance is an object of political decision and struggle. Within the broad parameters of a strategy based on these pro-capitalist principles there are many alternative approaches. In the past income maintenance has been influenced by the intervention of anti-capitalist political forces and certainly it will continue to be in the future. What we wish to highlight is that progressive forces have in the main only managed to affect the emphasis of policy within the confines of a broadly defined 'pro-capitalist' approach. Only occasionally have the principles of such an approach been seriously dented. Socialists have tended to assume income maintenance is a 'good thing', because it appears to embody values of communality and equality. The point that income maintenance can operate according to pro-capitalist principles has been largely ignored and the question of who benefits from particular measures has not been examined in detail. The left now finds itself without an adequate critique of the present system, at a time when its deficiencies are becoming more and more apparent to those who have to use it. The Tories are able to blame the left for the failures of a system which in fact owes more to the ideology of the right than that of the left. Moreover the left appears to have no positive answers to the obvious failings of the system: it is repeatedly pushed into a defensive posture in relation to Tory cuts. The position which the labour movement has taken up — arguing for a return to the principles of 1945 — provides few answers to the main contemporary problems: low pay; high housing costs; racism; sexism; inequalities in the state pension scheme; low incomes consequent on disability; the relationship between taxation and benefits; long-term mass unemployment. It is about time the left paid serious attention to questions which are relevant to today's income maintenance system: otherwise we will simply continue to get right-wing answers to left-wing questions.

Key Concepts

Public Services, Income Maintenance and Democracy

There is always a choice between service provision and income maintenance. If, for example, a disabled person needs help in getting around, the state can provide a mobility allowance which may help to pay for minicabs or go towards buying a car; alternatively, the state can provide a free taxi service for disabled people. In reality there may be a range of options, but the two extremes indicate the type of choice to be made. Socialists confronted with this dilemma generally tend to prefer the public service option. This preference has been a factor contributing to the lack of interest traditionally shown by the left in income maintenance issues, but there is very little consistency about it. Few socialists would propose replacing unemployment benefit with publicly run canteens and dormitories.

The key to resolving this problem is giving democratic control of the relationship between benefits and services to those affected. Disability provides a good example. The cost of paying benefit to a carer in the home and the cost of day-care services are linked. It is crucial that the balance between them is determined by disabled people themselves. Similar points apply to parents and childcare provision, to the unemployed and involvement in training and job creation, to tenants and public housing, and so on. A prerequisite of such democratic control is the integration of the administration of income maintenance with that of relevant service areas. It is apparent that local authorities are the only existing institutions which could come remotely near to integrating such functions under democratic control. But in general local authorities exclude from power those same groups — the unemployed, women, black people, disabled people, the low paid, the elderly — as are excluded by central government. The kind of democratic control which is required entails giving representation to these groups within the decision-making structure.

We have emphasized the importance of local democracy and the way in which income maintenance could contribute to its development. However, decisions on individual benefit entitlement must be largely free of such local democratic control. Local committees could not be allowed similar powers to those currently exercised by benefit officials. The individual claimant would land up at just as much of a disadvantage. The first consequence of this is that democratic power must extend up to the national level. There must be structures of representation within the income maintenance system itself through which claimants, and people on low incomes, can influence decisions on setting benefit and minimum wage levels, on the assessment of needs for cost-related benefits , on conditions applying to the payment of positional benefits, and so on. Secondly, these decisions must be enforced through a clear legal structure which guarantees the entitlement of individuals to benefits, and their rights to adequate information, to confidentiality, and to appeal against decision.

Decisions, Decisions...

The repugnance people feel towards means tests is a response to two things. Firstly, the technical structure leads to treatment of the claimant which is unfair. Secondly, relations of power have been established between claimants and officials in which claimants find their rights systematically undermined. If they wish to preserve their incomes, they must respond to every official demand for information, they must be prepared to face surveillance and harassment, and they must accept that any information given to or taken by benefit officers may be passed to a third party at will.

'Selectivity' links these two aspects of means tests. A means-tested system selects individuals to receive benefit on grounds of low income. In the present system each action taken by the individual which could result in a change of income becomes the basis of a new 'selection process'. The result is to push claimants into a state of dependancy on officials: everything they do must be reported and approved. This requirement to get approval doesn't apply only to changes of income. For SB purposes, other 'relevant' actions would include making a gift of money, going on holiday, undertaking voluntary work, or spending savings. Moreover, claimants have to report even those actions which are not in fact relevant to benefit assessments, just in case they might be: only officials (and professional advisers) have the key of knowledge to what is 'relevant'.

A precondition for redressing the balance of power between officials and claimants is to shift the burden of selectivity which currently falls on individuals within the income maintenance system. In some areas it is easy to shift this burden. Take the example of housing, which we discuss in detail in Chapter 7. Recent policy has been to put up rents so that they are out of the reach of most tenants. Meanwhile, another government minister is responsible for a complicated and inefficient system of Housing Benefit (HB), which reduces the rents of those on lowest incomes. The burden of selectivity can be shifted by adopting the opposite approach: guaranteeing a minimum income (through benefits and wages) and controlling rents, so that individual tenants can automatically afford their housing. The process of selective decision-making could then be applied to housing itself, not to its occupants. When and what type of new housing is needed? What housing requires improvement and renovation? These are the decisions that could be taken *by* tenants. Rather than being the objects of selectivity, they would be the ones making selections.

Even the Best Means Test in the World

We have considered in detail the question of power relations between claimants and officials. Some commentators suggest that this area of difficulty, usually described as 'administrative', is the only source of the unpopularity of means tests. They imply that there is no inherent difficulty with the idea of means-testing itself. The government may not be willing to take these ideas to their logical conclusion, but it certainly has been willing to exploit the implications of this argument: that means tests are an efficient and acceptable method of targeting benefits on those most in need. We reject this view and conclude that there are inherent objections to means tests, which go beyond issues of administration and relate to means-testing as a method of assessment.

Authors of an Institute of Fiscal Studies (IFS) book on income maintenance have used the example of the Duke of Westminster to ridicule the idea of paying benefits *without* means tests. Why should child benefit or retirement pension be paid to a man who owns roughly five hundred million pounds?[2] This point rests on a misunderstanding: it attributes to those who object to means-testing the assumption that the market must not be interfered with. Faced with a man who owns five hundred million pounds, they say, 'Let's save the £35.80 retirement pension and give it to the poor.' We would rather say, 'Let's take the £500 million and redistribute it. He can still claim retirement pension.' If one accepts the existing inequalities in income and wealth distribution, then of course means-testing is the only way of ensuring that nobody is destitute. But a socialist approach does not share that objective: on the contrary it rests on the belief that poverty can only be abolished *by reducing inequality*. Such an approach entails a direct intervention in the distribution of 'initial incomes' and of wealth, to ensure that every individual is assured of an initial income above the poverty level.

The IFS authors also argue that opposition to means-testing is based on superstition:

> It is clear that rational objection is not to means tests as such. The battle over whether the state could properly enquire into the resources of its citizens is one which was fought, vigorously, in the early nineteenth century when income tax was introduced ... No-one now disputes that this kind of investigation is both proper and necessary.

This point is gaining credibility in the political debate about income maintenance. It plays cleverly on the common perception that the current system is a complex mess, with a totally irrational relationship between social security and taxation. The problem is usually illustrated by pointing to people who get means-tested benefits and yet pay tax as well. So a low-paid worker may both receive family income supplement (FIS) and pay tax, and the effect of the two 'adjustments' to the worker's income may cancel each other out. In response to this situation, the IFS authors propose merging the tax and benefit systems, so that each individual would have just one adjustment made to their income, either up or down. If the worker's FIS benefit was greater than their tax liability, they would receive a payment (equal to FIS less tax); if the benefit entitlement was less than the tax liability, they would make a net payment to the state (tax less FIS). The analytic point arising out of such proposals is this: if such a merger is possible, can a valid distinction still be drawn between means-tested benefits — the crediting of an amount of money to the individual related to their other income — and taxation — the debiting of an amount of money from the individual related to their other income?

We believe it is valid to make such a distinction, and it can be illustrated by comparing the effect of means-testing and taxation as they apply to benefits themselves. Consider the example of two pensioners under the present system, one on supplementary pension which is means-tested, the other on retirement pension which is not means-tested but which is taxable. They both have occupational pensions. Let us consider what happens if in both cases their occupational pension goes up by £5 a week. The supplementary pensioner suffers a reduction in net state benefit: it goes down by £5, because the increased income from the occupational pension is taken into account in full. The retirement pensioner also suffers a reduction in net state benefit, but a lesser one: the person will still get the same amount of retirement pension (because it isn't means-tested), but they will pay more tax.

The example illustrates what the means-testing and taxation of benefits have in common: both ensure that as the claimant's other income increases the net benefit s/he gets from the state reduces. But it also illustrates the difference between means-testing and taxation. Means-testing makes this adjustment to the claimant's benefit according to rules which are *less favourable* than the rules applying to the simple taxation of income. So, in the example of the two pensioners, the supplementary pensioner suffers a rate of benefit withdrawal of a pound per pound, whereas the retirement pensioner may be losing only thirty pence for each pound by which their other income increases. This clearly demonstrates the problem with means-testing, even means-testing carried out in the fairest possible way. It treats poor people worse than other people.

The technical solutions such as those put forward by the IFS authors and by the Alliance parties, involving a mixture of benefit and tax credits which would nominally integrate benefits with taxation, would alleviate some of the worst irrationalities of the present system. But they would rigidly entrench the principle of means-testing at the very heart of income maintenance. People getting means-tested benefits would still be disadvantaged by experiencing 'tax rates' far in excess of those applied to the highest income earners. The state would still be conniving in the payment of wages below the subsistence level and would itself pay pensions below that level. It would then demand that the recipients of these inadequate incomes demand extra help from the state, knowing that the price of that extra help is the acceptance of a whole new set of rules to a game which everyone else considers too demeaning to play.

The infinitely preferable alternative is simple. The state must intervene directly to ensure that everyone starts with an income at least adequate to their needs, so that the only adjustments to that income are down (through taxation), not up (through a means test). Such a system could retain the principle of being based on individual needs by taking account of housing costs, disability and so on. Moreover, it could be redistributive through taxation and the provision of a minimum income to the unwaged. But we could consign the forms, regulations and secret instructions of means tests to the paper shredder.

Wages and Income Maintenance

It has become commonplace to argue that policies regarding social security should take account of the interrelationship of tax and benefits. But this is starting one step too late, if the interaction between wages, occupational welfare and social welfare is ignored. The interaction between the wages and income maintenance systems is complex. In our view any approach which attempts to deal with either system in isolation from the other is essentially flawed. This criticism applies equally to those trade unionists who base their whole strategy around 'free collective bargaining' and to reformers who propose changes to the benefits system without relating those changes to the wider context in which social welfare operates.

In their most basic form, the links between wages and income maintenance can be exposed by looking at what actually determines the incomes of the two groups apparently divided by the wages–welfare split. There is a majority non-employed population of pensioners, child-carers (including single parents), those incapable of work through sickness or disability, students, children, the unemployed and so on. Their incomes and real welfare are determined by levels of benefits and rules of entitlement; their own previous wages (if any), or those of a spouse (for example, because of the effect on a pension); relations of dependancy to and responsibility for any members of their immediate family — and the wages of those other members if they work; savings and other wealth; the availability of public services; the cost of living; their needs. The same set of factors determines the incomes and real welfare of the minority of the population in employment, except that now we must talk about their 'current' rather than 'previous' wages.

There are of course major distinctions to be drawn between wages and income maintenance. There are the material differences — in particular that wages are generally higher than benefit payments. There are also differences of principle, which can be summarized in this way: unlike benefits and taxes, wages are an exchange of money for work performed. Wages are generally set by a combination of market forces and negotiation, whereas income levels secured through income maintenance are set by state decisions. Yet even here caution is essential. It is too easy to assume that because the processes are distinct they are also unrelated. Aside from the general political and social environment which conditions wage negotiation (for example, mass unemployment), there is also a very specific 'fiscal' environment, as well as the forms of direct state intervention such as the incomes policy which currently operates in the public sector. Wage levels and increases are inevitably affected by such factors as what level of support is provided through benefits for children and the benefits payable to non-working spouses. Conversely, it would be hard to forget under a Tory government that benefit levels are set with wage levels very much in mind.

The picture is made more complex by the problem of the 'incidence' of taxes and benefits. The problem can be illustrated by looking at FIS. A parent who is in full-time work receives a FIS payment if her income drops below a certain level. Ostensibly the aim of FIS is to reduce the effect of low pay in causing family poverty. But employers may, over a period of time, reduce wages in the knowledge that the government will make up the difference through FIS. In that case FIS will in effect operate as a subsidy to employers paying low wages.

The same may happen if income tax is cut. Indeed, when Nigel Lawsón defends income tax cuts as a method of creating jobs, he does so on the basis that they cut *wage costs for employers* not on the basis that they increase workers' incomes. In practice, the effect of any change in income maintenance is mediated by a struggle between the parties involved and is therefore dependant on their relative strengths. In the current situation, it is likely that losses will be passed on to workers by employers, and gains retained by them. In a situation of full employment the reverse may occur.

In the light of this discussion, we reject the general concept of 'fiscal neutrality' which has become so fashionable among right-wing thinkers and which has won the heart of Nigel Lawson, the Chancellor. The idea is that the tax and benefit system should be reformed so that it does not 'distort' the free operation of market forces. But this is a fantasy: it is to wish away the existence of the state through whose hands more than 40 per cent of the Gross Domestic Product passes every year. This argument may be uncontroversial to most people on the left. But the corollary is less comfortable: that the concept of '*free* collective bargaining' is just as suspect as that of 'fiscal neutrality'. Collective bargaining takes place in a fiscal, economic and legal environment determined politically. Pretending this is not so is wishful thinking.

Poverty and Equality

A society which gave every individual the same income would not be equal. Individual needs vary: a disabled person is likely to need to spend more on transport than an able-bodied person. Costs for housing vary widely from area to area. Equality in the fullest sense would mean meeting the needs of individuals in the context of their social relationships, for example, the family and household in which they live and where they live (for example, distance from shopping centres or from work). Such needs would have to be met through a combination of public services and income maintenance.

Implicit in this argument is the view that needs are constituted socially and this is of much wider application: it underlies the notion of poverty. Often this view is stated in terms of the theory of 'relative deprivation'. The choice of phrase is unfortunate, seeming to suggest that people in Britain are only poor *relative* to the better off. It is then a short step to argue that there is no *real* hardship, or, as Paul Ashton has put it, 'Poverty, like beauty, is inevitably in the eye of the beholder.'[3]

When we say that needs — and therefore *any* poverty standard — are socially constituted, we are not stating that the poverty standard is some kind of upwardly mobile social climber, shifting according to the selfish whims of the poor who always want more of everything. We are saying that in a *real* sense needs change as society changes. According to the 'Breadline Britain' survey,[4] over three-quarters of people now believe that a fridge is an essential. This must be seen as the result of a variety of factors: changed living conditions (centrally heated homes without larders); changed food production; and the wide availability of fridges. There are also 'diswelfares' produced by technological and social change: for example, pollution causes diseases which require new forms of health care. These changing needs are not only perceived by the poor themselves or by people sympathetic to them, the changes are not 'in the eye of the beholder'. They are measurable, as the 'Breadline Britain' survey demonstrated by the simple and effective method of surveying the general population.[5]

To adopt an absolute poverty standard such as Beveridge's would be to refer the poor back to social conditions which no longer exist. Beveridge, in fact, based *his* standard on research undertaken by Rowntree in York in the 1890s and updated in the 1930s. Are claimants therefore to entertain themselves in music halls and to feed on the diet of the Victorian age? Or should social security be frozen for ever at 1948 levels, giving claimants enough money to buy rationed egg powder and ersatz coffee, and to attend the 'picture house' once a week — but not to buy a TV licence?

Certainly poverty is inextricably linked to inequality, and serious measures to reduce poverty must tackle the problem of inequality. An unequal society will always prevent a large number of people from satisfying their needs — needs which that society itself creates through social and economic structures which impose a particular way of living on individuals. There are now a large number of people in Britain whose incomes are so low that they cannot afford several items which most people believe to be essential and who are thereby denied any 'normal' level of participation in society. Moreover the number of people in this predicament has been growing steadily in recent years. This is the problem that must be addressed.

Poverty and Income Maintenance

The correct approach to measuring poverty has often been confused with the best way of reducing it. In general terms, if it is accepted that poverty and inequality are closely linked, then an approach which simply seeks to raise those on the lowest incomes up to a subsistence level of income (the poverty standard) is only directed at half the problem. The idea of means-testing is precisely this — to top up those incomes which fall below the poverty line. The more means tests have gained in importance in British social security, the more intractable the problem of poverty has become.

There are also more specific problems which arise from using the idea of poverty as the basis of income maintenance policy. The first source of difficulty is that the measurement of poverty ignores the all-important *causes* of inadequate incomes. If you are on a low income because you have given up work to look after your children, then the question is whether the state should support you in carrying out that caring role. If you have a low income because you are in work and low paid, then the question is whether that's your responsibility, in which case you should join a union or get retrained; or your employer's responsibility, in which case they should be forced to pay you adequately; or the state's responsibility, in which case you should be paid benefits.

All income maintenance payments are based on an evaluation of average needs. The second problem with poverty-standard benefits is that they set this average at a subsistence level. Since Beveridge this principle has never seriously been challenged. But if benefits are set at subsistence level, those with above-average needs who claim benefits will still be deprived. If the objective is to eliminate poverty, there is then a choice: the basic level of benefit can be raised; or particular cost-related benefits can be introduced to deal with variations in individual needs. There is a trade-off: the higher the 'subsistence' benefits, the less need for selectively determined cost-related benefits. The final problem is that poverty standards traditionally relate to the family. Once again, this tends to obscure the real issues. The idea of the family centres on the responsibility of the breadwinner to support 'his' dependants. Consequently the issue of social responsibility for those without wages is fudged.

Our response to these problems is to move away from the use of poverty standards as the basis of income maintenance. Rather than attempting to top up incomes to reach a poverty standard, income maintenance should be related to the causes of low incomes and to a political view of responsibilities for them. On this basis, we advocate that the state should not top up low wages through benefits, but should enforce a responsibility on employers to pay an adequate minimum wage. In turn the state should recognize a responsiblity for those in positions where they do not have wages: it should pay 'positional benefits' to pensioners, the sick, carers and the unemployed and so on. Finally, the level of benefits and the minimum wage should be set at a level above subsistence, so that the need for cost-related benefits is kept at a minimum and the redistributive impact of income maintenance is maximized.

Our approach does not limit income maintenance to those on the lowest incomes. Those solutions which have attempted to eradicate poverty by concentrating help in this way have only succeeded in reproducing it. Instead we propose tackling poverty at its roots — the sources of inequality.

36

The Principles of a Socialist Approach

We now turn to consider the principles which we believe should underlie a socialist approach to income maintenance. Many of them follow directly from the criticisms we made in the first part of this chapter of the principles underpinning the current system of welfare, and others are derived from the discussion of key concepts in the second part. The next six chapters discuss the practical implications of these principles and the types of policies which would be necessary to achieve them. The principles provide the framework for a socialist approach to income maintenance and could point the way to a series of radical reforms which, taken together, would be a substantial contribution to the achievement of a socialist society. These are the ten principles:

(1) *Income maintenance should have as its overriding goals the meeting of needs and the reduction of inequality.* It is clear that greater equality must be one of the fundamental aims of socialist politics. The claim that socialism can produce a fairer society — both in terms of incomes and the distribution of power — is the main claim socialism has on popular support. Income maintenance policies are the most important element of an egalitarian politics. A programme for achieving greater equality must encompass a programme for meeting individual needs, as the two objectives are identical. Thus greater equality entails that some groups would receive higher incomes — for example, disabled people would receive supplements in respect of their special needs.

Another consequence of this general principle is that income maintenance must aim for the equalization of minimum incomes between the employed and the non-employed. This aspect of equality may have to be seen as a long-term objective. Nevertheless, in principle, we can see no long-term justification for paying the non-employed lower minimum incomes than the employed.

(2) *Employers have a responsibility to meet the needs of their employees at a socially determined level.* The state would make it clear that paying decent wages is the responsibility of employers. The state should intervene to compel employers to meet that responsibility through a statutory minimum wage. It may also choose to subsidize some enterprises and forms of production in a planned fashion. But the question of responsibility for the costs of employment should not be fudged, as it is at present, by the payment of means-tested benefits to supplement low wages.

(3) *The payment of benefits should be based on a social definition of the state's responsibility for those without wages and for those who face exceptional expenditure on day-to-day living.* 'Positional benefits' would be paid to those without wages for reasons such as caring responsibilities, sickness or unemployment. Cost-related benefits

would meet exceptional costs caused, for example, by high rents. In our view these two categories provide for the full range of needs for which the state should accept responsibility through benefits. This approach would make explicit the responsibilities which the state accepts and those which it refuses; it therefore allows clear political decisions to be taken about those responsibilities. For example, the state has an obligation to guarantee people an adequate income if they are unable to take paid employment because they are providing this care at home. Similarly, the state should accept responsibility for ensuring that people can afford to house themselves adequately.

(4) *All individuals should have the right and responsibility to participate in economic and social life.* The crucial point here is the enshrinement of a right as well as a responsibility. Traditionally, the income maintenance system has been content to use the responsibility to participate — by working — as a test to be applied to a particular group of claimants, the unemployed. So reactionary has been the administration of this rule that it is tempting simply to advocate its abolition. However, we believe there is an underlying principle which is central to the development of a socialist society — individuals must be prepared to contribute to society. The difference in a socialist approach is that it places an equal responsibility on the state to attempt to provide full employment and to support individuals during spells of unemployment. Secondly, a socialist approach would not restrict the general principle to the unemployed, although obviously the details of its operation differ for different groups. It seems to us that the state must accept a responsibility for ensuring that disabled people and the elderly can participate in economic life, both by tailoring income maintenance rules to make this possible and by creating employment opportunities suitable to the needs of disabled and elderly people. Moreover, the state should attempt to ensure that all members of society have sufficient income to enable them to participate fully in the life of the community. The levels of benefits and of the minimum wage should not be linked to a subsistence standard, but should be based on the social conditions and needs which exist today. Benefit levels should enable even those with above average needs to participate to a reasonable level.

(5) *There should be no contributory or earnings-related benefits.* This principle follows directly from the commitment to the satisfaction of needs. Contribution tests are often defended on the grounds of their popularity and their function in legitimating social security. People are said to feel justified in drawing benefits because they 'have paid something in'. This may be true, but there is an unacceptable price to pay. If people feel justified in drawing a pension because they contributed to it, they are also bound to look down on the pensioner who gets benefit without having made adequate contributions. Secondly, there is no

point in having contribution tests unless someone loses from them. But if someone does lose, then benefits are being assessed on criteria other than needs. The same arguments apply to earnings-related benefits, but in addition they are more finely discriminatory.

(6) *Means tests should be abolished.* We have explained earlier in the chapter what we mean by 'means tests', in contrast to the taxation of benefits. In a system without means tests, any particular rules regarding the taxation of benefits would be at least as favourable as the taxation rules for other forms of income.

(7) *Income maintenance should be assessed on an individual basis, and relations of dependancy should not be assumed between adults.* This is essential in giving dignity and freedom to all members of society, irrespective of sex or marital status. It is also essential to the abolition of poverty, unless that project is to rest on the shaky ground of the voluntary redistribution of incomes within the family. When people say that this basic principle (often called 'disaggregation') is too costly, they should remember this: the entire population needs supporting and supposedly is supported now. The opponents of 'separate treatment' want to have their cake and eat it. If it is argued that men already provide an adequate level of support to women within the family, then they have nothing material to lose by giving those women the dignity of an independent income. If men do not in fact provide that level of support, then women are financially disadvantaged and the case for reform is overwhelming. The issue is one of power, not resources. It is also a question of the freedom of women receiving benefit to form relationships or to share housing with whom they like — without financial penalties on them or their children.

(8) *There should be equality of treatment between sexes, races and localities.* This principle speaks for itself and would probably not be seriously disputed even by non-socialists. Yet, as we saw in the last chapter, the present system discriminates on all three counts. The achievement of this goal entails the abolition of residence conditions and the abolition of local discretion, for example, in educational welfare and HB 'local schemes'. It also entails separate assessment (see (7) above), and the abolition of contribution tests (5). It does not necessarily rule out regional variations in income maintenance if these relate to genuine variations in needs or costs.

(9) *Everyone should have the right to claim benefits with privacy, dignity and confidentiality, without fear of harassment, and with an adequate right of redress.* The administration of income maintenance is a key issue. At the moment the rights of claimants are abused at every turn. Protecting the rights of claimants means that the rules must be simple and readily comprehensible. We should expect the

same standard of service in relation to income maintenance as from any service to the public. The standard of confidentiality traditionally expected by individuals receiving health care is a good basis for comparison.

(10) *Income maintenance should be democratically controlled and should be compatible with the development of democratic decision making.* It is crucial to the socialist ideal that income maintenance should always be compatible with, and should encourage the development of, democratic ways of expressing and meeting needs. It is also crucial that income maintenance itself should become more susceptible to local democratic control, in order to redress the imbalance of power between claimants and officials. The burden of selectivity must be shifted away from individuals in order to open up other areas of social and economic life to democratic scrutiny and control. For example, moving from the use of means-tested benefits for those in work to a minimum wage allows for the democratic control of subsidies to go to particular enterprises; it therefore permits the socialist question: is this particular form of enterprise suited to the needs of the community? Rather than being selective about the needs of individuals, let us, for a change, be selective about the needs of businesses. Not surprisingly, the effect of a largely means-tested system of benefits is to blame individuals, to confuse causes and to obstruct democratic solutions. Our aims must be opposed to these at every stage.

Notes

1. The state can intervene to reduce costs without predetermining who the individual beneficiary will be, if two or more people are jointly liable for a charge. Housing benefit rebated from a council rent where there are joint tenants is one example.

2. AW Dilnot, JA Kay and CN Morris, *The Reform of Social Security*, Oxford 1984.

3. Paul Ashton, 'Poverty and Its Beholders', *New Society*, 18 October 1984.

4. Stewart Lansley and Joanna Mack, *Poor Britain*, London 1985.

5. Ibid.

3
Unemployment and Low Pay

It is easy to fall into the trap of thinking of employment issues in terms of two stark alternatives: either you are one of the 'lucky ones' who has a secure full-time job, or you are part of the unfortunate minority, the unemployed. This picture has never been accurate. It always represented a particularly 'male' view of work. Recent developments have made the picture less — not more — true. Over the last few years the number of full-time employees has dropped rapidly, not just because of the growth of mass unemployment, but also because of the increase in part-time work, self-employment and various forms of special temporary employment (such as Manpower Services Commission schemes). In 1983, out of a total population of working age of 33.3 million, slightly less than half (16 million) were employed full-time. Among men the proportion was slightly higher, 63 per cent. But less than a third of women were employed full-time (5 million), only slightly more than the number of part-time workers (4 million); a further 5.1 million women were categorized as 'economically inactive', that is, mainly unpaid child-carers and domestic labourers.

There is an accelerated tendency towards a more divided labour market. First, there are full-time employees with permanent jobs, generally better conditions of employment, often in private pension schemes, frequently unionized. Secondly, there are part-time workers, people on government training schemes, workers employed by sub-contractors to the larger firms, home-workers and the self-employed undertaking work for such firms. All of these tend to have fewer rights, undertake more routinized tasks and are less likely to be unionized. Finally, there are the unemployed, forced to subsist on the lowest incomes: if they do get any work, they are often forced to accept insecure low-status employment. These developments, however, should not obscure the fact that such divisions have always existed in a lesser form: divisions between organized and unorganized workers, whites and blacks, men and women, those working and those not working. These divisions have always been reflected in and reinforced by inequalities of income. For example, women have always been low paid or not paid at all; black workers have received lower wages and have been thrown on to the mercies of the dole in proportionately greater numbers than whites.

In one sense, the basic structure of income maintenance is well adapted to the creation and reinforcement of these divisions in the labour market. It is in many respects a two-status income maintenance system. The binary principle of benefits imposes a distinction between those who need only claim insurance benefits and those who have to subject themselves to the means test. This distinction has been emphasized by developments of the basic income maintenance structure: historically, by the introduction of state earnings-related benefits, and now by the increasing encouragement to private provision. Higher-status workers are more likely to avoid means tests by getting higher wages in work, by staying in employment and by accruing rights to private or state earnings-related pensions in retirement. Other workers and the unemployed face low wages, together with means tests in work, in unemployment and in retirement.

Tory policy has been directed at encouraging these divisions in the labour force. Their strategy has been to increase the profits of entrepreneurs and businesses by reducing wage costs and by making it more easy to hire and fire workers, to take on workers on temporary contracts, etc. This strategy has involved a coordinated attack on those in and out of work. New legislation has reduced the statutory protection of individual employees and the freedom of trade unions to organize collectively.

The labour movement has a poor record on these issues. The Labour Party in power did not effectively deal with the question of inequality in employment or between the jobless and the employed. A socialist strategy to reverse the processes of stratification and impoverishment must grasp the complexity of the relationship between the labour market and income maintenance. Unemployment, the low level of benefits (to the employed and the unemployed), low pay and rights in employment, all these are linked issues which require an integrated approach. In this chapter we will show how a socialist income maintenance strategy would fit with the necessary kind of integrated approach to employment issues. Moreover such a strategy could form the basis of an alliance between groups currently frequently divided politically as well as socially.

Income Maintenance and the Labour Market Now

Low Pay: Government Intervention

Traditionally, governments have at least gone through the motions of treating low pay as a problem, even if the solutions adopted have often lacked the conviction necessary to make them successful. It is useful to review the particular solutions which have been tried, and some of the reasons why they have never succeeded in eradicating low pay:

(1) *Statutory Minimum Wage Rates.* Since 1909, minimum wage rates have been set for specific industries by statutory bodies (first the trade boards and now wage councils). Around 3 million workers in industries such as hairdressing, catering, laundries and clothing manufacture are covered by wage council orders.

Effect: wage councils have always been toothless bodies only covering a small minority of workers. There are currently only 119 wages inspectors to enforce wage council rates and there is no obligation on employers to register with them so their records are hopelessly out of date. The wage orders are complicated and hard to get hold of and the rates of pay are set at such a low level that, even if employers do comply, their workers may still be low paid.

(2) *Statutory Support for Collective Bargaining.* In the past, governments have provided statutory support for collective bargaining. For example, Schedule 11 of the Employment Protection Act 1975 allowed workers to claim higher wages if they could show they were being paid less than the going rate for the job. The Fair Wages Resolution (introduced by a Conservative government in 1891) stopped government departments from subcontracting work to any firms which did not operate recognized wage agreements.

Effect: Following their abolition by the Tories, conditions of employment in public sector subcontracting have deteriorated markedly. This suggests that these measures did in fact have an important effect in limiting exploitation.

(3) *Statutory Measures Against Discrimination.* Governments have — in appearance at least — acted to eliminate discrimination in pay and employment through the Equal Pay Act and the Sex and Race Discrimination Acts.

Effect: equal pay legislation has had some impact on sexual inequalities, but has still left women earning on average around 74 per cent of what their male counterparts earn.[1] Action against race discrimination has been similarly ineffective. The legislation places the main responsibility for countering discrimination on those who experience it. Tribunals and courts have adopted highly restrictive interpretations of the law, and the penalties which they can impose are an inadequate deterrent.

(4) *Employment Protection Measures.* Limited employment protection — against unfair dismissal and victimization — has been afforded to workers. Employment protection measures are clearly essential if statutory measures against low pay are to have any success. Workers must have the confidence to make complaints against their employers, without fear of dismissal.

Effect: The current provisions do not provide that kind of protection, especially given the unwillingness of industrial tribunals to order reinstatement rather than compensation. But, in any case, employment protection is only effective against low pay in combination with other successful measures.

(5) *Means-tested Benefits.* Governments of both parties have shown themselves increasingly in favour of 'solving' the problem of low pay by allowing it to continue and paying benefits to the workers suffering the effects.

Effect: Apart from offering limited assistance to some of the victims of low pay, the main effect of means-tested benefits appears to be to legitimize and even encourage low wages. Employers are able to point out that the state apparently guarantees that workers do not fall below the 'subsistence line', no matter how badly paid, and indeed that a wage increase may not benefit the worker much or at all after taxes have been paid and benefits reduced as a result.

Arguably these measures have not reflected a real intention of eliminating low pay, so much as an attempt to provide a 'wage floor' to underpin the wage structure. Since 1979, the Tories have abandoned even this limited objective. Continually asserting that the low paid are 'pricing themselves out of jobs' — unlike the high paid who apparently can't price themselves too highly — the government has set about actively encouraging employers to pay badly. Ministers frequently quote the statistic that average pay has risen above the level of inflation as an indication of the need to weaken trade unions. But the average figure is misleading. Between 1980 and 1984 average earnings went up faster than the earnings of low-paid workers. During this period the index of prices for the low paid also rose faster than the retail price index. In fact low-paid men suffered a real wage cut in this period and the real earnings of low-paid women virtually stood still.[2]

The government has been particularly vindictive in its approach to young people. Astonishingly, the Young Workers' Scheme (YWS) pays a subsidy (of £15 a week) for each sixteen- or seventeen-year-old employed at a wage *less than* £50 a week, even though in some cases this is less than the legal minimum rate set by the appropriate wage council. The Tories have considered a proposal to stop paying Supplementary Benefit (SB) to those young people who refuse places on Youth Training Schemes (YTS), schemes which pay only £26.25 a week to trainees and provide a growing pool of cheap labour. YTS trainees are regarded as employed by the Department of Employment so that they do not figure in the unemployment statistics. But the DHSS denies them industrial injury benefits on the grounds they are 'not employed'. The proposal would complete the process of making school-leavers non-people as far as the government is concerned: not employed, not unemployed, and not claimants.

Young people suffer a far more severe problem of low pay than adults. In April 1984, a third of full-time women workers aged under eighteen earned less than £50 a week gross.[3] The West Midlands Low Pay Unit has come across some employers whose work-force now consists *entirely* of YTS 'trainees' and YWS workers. The employer pays the YTS trainees nothing, and some of the YWS workers are paid as low as £28 for a forty-hour week, with a £15 government subsidy. One timber merchant had a staff of thirty-five — fifteen on YWS and twenty on YTS.[4]

The effect of the abolition of the Fair Wages Resolution which guaranteed union rates on government contracts has been dramatic. Until 1 November 1984, fifty-nine cleaners employed by Pritchard Services to clean government offices in Durham used to receive £1.80 an hour plus four weeks' holiday. Little enough, but under the new contract negotiated between Pritchard and the government their pay has been reduced to £1.40 an hour and their holiday entitlement to one week. On top of this there have been ten redundancies, increasing the workload of those 'lucky' to still have a job by about 17 per cent. According to John Hall, Secretary General of the Contract Cleaning and Maintenance Association, this is not an isolated incident: 'It is fair to say that pay rates being quoted in Government Departments at the present time are 20% lower than they were before.'[5]

The government has also attempted further to undermine the wage councils. In August 1983, Norman Tebbit (then the Employment Secretary) wrote to the catering industry wage council opposing an annual increase in workers' pay of 9p an hour to £1.63 an hour; he said it would be 'harmful to business and jobs'.[6] Of those employers visited by wage inspectors in 1983, 37 per cent were found to be under-paying at least some of their workers. Yet legal action was only taken against seven employers — five civil actions for recovery of arrears, and just two criminal prosecutions.[7] Not content with the feebleness of this performance and the confirmation of the fact that wage councils are widely ignored anyway, the government has been actively considering abolishing them altogether.[8]

Despite the government's headstrong persistence in arguing for lower and lower wages, there is actually little evidence to support their contention that increased exploitation of low-paid workers will create jobs. Henry Neuburger, a former Treasury economist, has calculated the effects of wage council abolition.[9] Although abolition would significantly lower some wage rates, it would create a negligible increase in jobs.[10] Using the Treasury's own computer model, Neuburger found that abolition would result in only 8,000 extra jobs after five years.

This is really not surprising. The government's strategy of creating low-paid jobs in 'no-tech' industries amounts to attempting to compete in price terms with economies such as Taiwan's. Abysmally low as wage council rates are — for example, 76p an hour for a first-year apprentice hairdresser — wages will have to drop a lot further before they undercut Third World competition. In fact it is hard to believe that the government is really serious in putting forward its strategy for job creation. In reality it is a strategy for increasing social divisions and private profits, rather than a genuine approach to the problems of unemployment and of poverty among workers.

Who Is Low Paid Now?

After six years of Tory policies, low pay has become a problem of massive proportions. According to the Low Pay Unit's definition of low pay, there are currently 8.3 million low-paid workers in Britain. Despite the huge figure that results, their definition is actually quite a moderate one: a gross weekly wage (before tax and other deductions) of £107 per week. Low pay for part-time workers is defined as an equivalent hourly rate, £2.75 per hour. This definition is actually lower than that proposed by the Council of Europe.[11] Low-paid workers are concentrated in manual occupations and in clerical and other low-grade office jobs.

Race discrimination has forced black workers into low-paying jobs. Black workers are concentrated in the lowest-paying sectors such as the textile and other manufacturing industries. In 1977, the proportions of economically active men and women whose occupations were manual were as follows: white, 52.9 per cent; Caribbean, 71.5 per cent; Indian, 63.7 per cent; Pakistani and Bangladeshi, 82.3 per cent.[12] A more recent survey showed that whereas more than a third of white male workers are in supervisory positions, less than a fifth of black male workers achieve such status. White male full-timers earn on average 17 per cent more than their black counterparts.[13]

There is little apparent inequality between the average earnings of black and white women, but this is not because black women have succeeded in winning better pay. On the contrary, it simply reflects the fact that white women are badly paid too. Women make up over two-thirds of all low-paid workers. Three-quarters of part-time women workers are low paid (on the hourly rate definition), that is, 3.2 million workers. In April 1984, the average earnings of part-time adult women workers were £39.70 (under £2.10 per hour).[14] Home-workers are among the worst-paid workers of all, with wage rates often falling below a pound an hour. In 1982 it was estimated that there were a quarter of a million homeworkers in England and Wales and that 71 per cent of them were women. Home-working is thought to be growing: partly because it allows managements to cut wage costs and partly because it is concentrated in the expanding non-manual and service sectors.[15]

The problems that even women in trade unions face in trying to free themselves from the low-pay trap are illustrated by the experience of women sewing-machinists at Ford. In 1968 three hundred women went on strike demanding equal pay with men doing jobs requiring equivalent skills. Although the job required five years' training, the workers complained that they were trained as unskilled within Ford's pay structure. The strike was settled when an inquiry was set up and Barbara Castle offered the unions the Equal Pay Act. But neither the inquiry nor the legislation led to the women being regraded. In 1984 the union took a case under the new provision of the Equal Pay Act (introduced to comply with EEC law) requiring 'equal pay for equal value', but even that failed. So sixteen years after the original dispute the women found themselves on strike over the same issue. Their shop steward, Lil Thompson, said the strike was not simply about the extra money, but about forcing the company to recognize women's skills: 'The reason we are in this grade is simple; it's because we are women.'[16] In April 1985 the women finally won their equal pay claim through an arbitration award, but only as a result of a long and determined struggle.

Unemployment

When the Conservatives first gained office, they argued that the unemployed lacked incentives to work. They therefore pursued a policy of widening the gap between those in and out of work. Six years later, we are told that low-paid workers are pricing themselves out of jobs by asking for too much. The object of the ideological attack appears to have changed, but the underlying themes are the same. Cash incentives are seen as all-important by the Tories; but whereas enhancing incentives entails increasing the incomes of the rich, it always implies reducing the living standards of the poor, whether working or unemployed.

For single people, unemployment generally means surviving on £28.05 SB a week. This is a weekly income with which the unemployed are supposed not only to clothe, feed and heat themselves, but also to keep in touch with society outside the dole queue and the post office. Two unemployed people living together as a couple get even less SB — £45.55 between them. Unemployment benefit was originally intended to be the main form of income support for those out of work. However, it lasts for only one year and is conditional on the claimant having paid enough National Insurance contributions in the right financial year. As a result the majority of unemployed people are not entitled to unemployment benefit. It is also currently paid at a level only 40p above the SB rate for a single person. So less than a quarter of unemployed people rely on unemployment benefit alone, without any SB 'top-up' (see Table 3.1).

The majority of even those 684,000 claimants who were getting unemployment benefit without SB would probably be topping it up with Housing Benefit (HB) instead. The insurance principle has been virtually abolished on the quiet as far as the unemployed are concerned and replaced with a dual means test, supplementary and housing benefit.

Table 3.1
WHAT BENEFITS DO THE OFFICIALLY UNEMPLOYED GET?

	Number (thousands)	%
Women		
Total	855	100
Unemployment Benefit only	283	33.1
Supplementary Benefit only	384	44.91
Unemployment and Supplementary Benefit	29	3.4
No benefit	158	18.48
Men		
Total	2,030	100
Unemployment Benefit only	401	19.75
Supplementary Benefit only	1,219	60.05
Unemployment and Supplementary Benefit	192	9.46
No benefit	218	10.74

Source: *Social Security Statistics 1984*, London 1984. Figures at November 1983.

So far we've only considered the position as it affects the three and a third million people (the January 1985 figure) officially recognized as unemployed. But a sensible approach seems to be to treat as unemployed anyone under pensionable age who is physically capable of working, who is not in full-time education, who wants a job and can't find one. On this basis, the current unemployment level is probably around 5 million — or around 15 per cent of the total population of working age. The government has managed to get this figure down by a mixture of blatant fiddles, phoney 'training programmes' and traditionally sexist assumptions about non-working women:[17] Indeed it is probable that even the 5 million figure only scratches the surface of unemployment — because it doesn't include the many women who are neither signing on as unemployed nor actively looking for work, but who would probably work if jobs and suitable child-care were available. The 'Breadline Greenwich' survey found that over half (52.7 per cent) of working-age women in the borough were neither working nor signing on as unemployed. Of these, nearly two-thirds gave child-care as a reason for not registering. Only 5 per cent said they didn't want to work.[18]

So what do the 2 million or more unemployed people who don't appear in the benefit statistics live on? The income maintenance system doesn't treat them as worthy of an income at all. These people are classed as 'economically inactive' by the government — and 77 per cent are women.[19] They have to rely on hand-outs from other members of their families.

As with so many other causes of poverty, the evidence shows that unemployment affects black people disproportionately. A Home Office research study in 1981 found that black workers are disproportionately affected by rises in the level of unemployment; moreover they consistently suffer higher levels of unemployment than white workers. These findings are borne out by the most recent survey conducted by the Department of Employment (see Table 3.2).

Table 3.2
THE PROPORTION OF 'ECONOMICALLY ACTIVE' MEN AND WOMEN IN ETHNIC GROUPS WHO ARE UNEMPLOYED (%)

	Men	Women
All ethnic origins	12.1	10.4
White	11.6	10.1
West Indian or Guyanese	27.6	18.0
Indian, Pakistani or Bangladeshi	21.5	21.6
Other	16.4	14.6

Source: *Labour Force Survey*, London 1983.

Another survey in 1983 found that 29 per cent of black men (excluding students and those permanently unable to work) had experienced at least one spell of unemployment in the previous twelve months.[20]

Incentives

Policy strategists on the right have succeeded in bringing the question of cash incentives to the forefront of discussions about the social security system. So much so that anomalies resulting from the interaction of social security and taxation have become popularly identified as the number one priority for reform. The government feels obliged to present policies as if the incentives issue was of real concern. The rate of benefit paid to ordinary claimants (after one year) cannot be paid to the unemployed, because it would raise their incomes too near to the lowest wage levels; too many workers get benefits and pay tax, so housing benefit must be cut back and tax allowances raised. These policies are in fact more coherently explained according to another logic: they reduce the expenditure on benefits and allow the money saved to be spent on tax cuts which disproportionately favour the rich.[21]

The relationship between incentives and benefits is usually described in terms of two 'traps': the unemployment trap and the poverty trap. The unemployment trap is said to arise because benefit rates are so near to the lowest wage rates that some workers — especially those with several dependants — may be better off on benefit than in work. It is asserted that they therefore might refuse offers of full-time jobs. But in 1983 only 2.9 per cent of those who had been unemployed for thirteen weeks were getting within 10 per cent of the incomes they had been getting when working: on average their income level when unemployed was only 60 per cent of their income level when working. After a year's unemployment, it had dropped to 53.2 per cent.[22] What is more, if the problem is supposed to be an economic one, all the evidence points to the fact that the unemployed are willing to take any jobs going. There are simply not enough jobs.

The poverty trap affects workers who both pay tax and get means-tested benefits. Out of each pound they earn, they lose not only 39p in tax and National Insurance but also a chunk of their benefits — as much as 69p more if they get both Family Income Supplement (FIS) and HB. Yet they're still expected to pay rent and fuel price increases. As with the unemployment trap the problem has generally been conceived as applying to full-time workers. Calculations based on the 1981 Family Expenditure Survey indicate that at that time only 2 per cent of families headed by a full-time worker would lose more than 50p for each extra pound earned. The poverty trap is in fact as likely to affect any household in which the sole worker is part-time, because so many of them are low paid. Since 1981 HB cuts combined with reductions in the relative earnings of the lowest paid will have made the problem of the poverty trap more widespread. But, once again, no evidence has been put forward that it is adversely affecting productivity or economic efficiency.

Both of these traps are unfair — on those who are unemployed and want to get work, and on workers on low pay. They impose a rate of 'taxation' on additional income higher than that which the Tories described as unacceptable — and which they abolished — for the rich. But the 'concern' expressed by the right on these issues does not address these questions.

The focus on incentives is a cover for the real economic policies of the Tory government, which are to impose benefit and wage cuts. This conclusion is supported by the evidence that the unemployed are desperate to find work, no matter how poor the pay and conditions, and that the low paid cling on to their jobs in preference to life on the dole. The experience of privatization — as in the example of Pritchard's discussion on p.45 — has been that people struggle against worsening conditions, but there is never a shortage of workers who will accept employment under the new conditions offered. The Thatcherite philosophy has, in any case, got people wrong: they are prepared to work for rewards other than simply cash. The willingness of the unemployed and the low paid to contribute should not be abused by yet more cuts in their living standards. On the contrary, the process should be reversed.

Responses

Bargaining Is Best?

Traditional trade union methods have not successfully dealt with the problems of the low paid and do not seem to offer much to them. This is a consequence of the suspicion with which unions have in the past treated legal intervention in employment matters. Jack Dromey (of the Transport and General Workers' Union) summed up the traditional approach when at a consultative conference called by the Trades Union Congress on low pay he argued that legal interference might weaken trade unions and that strong union organization and collective bargaining were the best ways of tackling low pay.[23] In November 1984 the TUC reasseted its strategy of attempting to achieve a wage target of two-thirds average male earnings through collective bargaining.[24] The problem with this strategy is that it ignores one of the major underlying causes of low pay: the workers affected often aren't in trade unions at all and, when they are, they don't have the industrial power to negotiate adequate conditions. The Grunwick dispute was an example of how the union movement has sometimes been unable to deliver the goods by this method alone, mainly because of the difficulties of applying union organizational methods to a small low-paid work-force faced by an intransigent management.

A new response is also required in relation to benefits. The traditional union attitude has been to support the extension of contributory benefits. The basis of this view is that insurance benefits favour those in work and earnings-related benefits favour the better paid. Therefore this strategy is arguably consistent with defending the interests of union members, who are in work, and strengthening the structure of collective bargaining. But there are two drawbacks. First, it is a fundamentally divisive strategy, since it favours those with jobs at the expense of those without. It therefore weakens the ability of workers to resist political and economic attack. Secondly, with mass unemployment, the contributory principle becomes less and less relevant even to union members, for reasons described above. The introduction of the 'notional strike pay' deduction in 1980 also highlighted the weakness of the union stance on these issues. The measure went through Parliament with barely any protest. It was only during the 1984/5 miners' strike that awareness of the importance of the change spread through the labour movement.

Some unions have always recognized these problems and there are now signs that more are responding to them. The principle of legal intervention in employment issues has always been welcomed and campaigned for in some areas, such as health and safety at work legislation. Unions such as the National Union of Public Employees representing lower-paid workers have moved towards a position of support for a legally enforced minimum wage. It is increasingly recognized that a statutory minimum wage would not undermine the trade union movement. A statutory minimum would operate as a base line below which no worker could drop; it would not diminish the effectiveness of unions in bargaining for better pay. For example, in France in 1979 only 4 per cent of the work-force received the statutory minimum.[25]

Those groups which predominantly experience the problems of low pay are chronically under-represented on decision-making bodies throughout the union movement. Despite the fact that women make up 43 per cent of the work-force and 31 per cent of union membership, they are not given equal status within the movement. In 1983 women made up the majority of the membership in six major unions, but the proportion of full-time officials who were women in each of those six unions ranged from 3.6 per cent (Association of Professional, Executive, Clerical, and Computer Staff) to 19.1 per cent (National Union of Tailoring and Garment Workers).[26] Nevertheless there is at least one hopeful sign, in that the NUTGW, operating in one of the lowest-paid industries, now has an executive half of whose members are women and which is chaired by a woman. Black workers are under-represented to an even greater degree. If the trade union movement is to draw these groups in on an active basis, as it must do if it is to renew its strength, it has to offer realistic solutions to their problems.

That means campaigning for a legally enforced minimum wage as well as for measures which support the role of unions and collective bargaining. It also means campaigning for the right of the unemployed to a decent income without tests of contributions or means, and abandoning the traditional support for the insurance principle. Finally, it means campaigning for reforms of the benefits system which will enable people to work part-time without having to accept a poverty income as a result. We are not suggesting that trade unions should abandon those of their members who have secure reasonably paid full-time employment. But defending their interests effectively requires the ability to mount an effective challenge to the Tory strategy of using unemployment as a weapon to lower wages. A labour movement united in its defence of those who are worst off in society would pose a real threat to the Tories, because the immorality of Tory politics would become the object of political debate.

Benefits or Wages?

We have made it clear that we believe the central solution to the problem of low pay must be a statutory minimum wage. An alternative option which has gained some ground both on the left and the right is the social credit or 'basic income guarantee'. For brevity in this discussion we will refer to this proposal as the 'Basic Income Guarantee' or BIG. This is the proposal to pay every adult, irrespective of their employment status or other income, a tax-free benefit at subsistence level. In theory at least, people would be free to be unemployed, or work full-or part-time; they would simply have to pay tax on their earnings. In Chapter 8 we will examine the technical aspects of the proposal; here we will examine the issues of principle.

Were it technically feasible to introduce BIG, would it be desirable? Our answer is, emphatically no. The scheme would be doing explicitly and on a larger scale what the present system of means-tested benefits for people in work does on the sly, that is, providing an indiscriminate subsidy to wages. As a general principle, employers should be compelled to meet the costs of employing the labour from which they derive a benefit. A minimum wage enforces that responsibility. There is no way of knowing how the subsidy proposed by BIG would be spent by employers — whether it would be spent on employing more workers, on investment, machinery or profits.

For the same reason, BIG would make the introduction of any form of economic planning that much more difficult. It is claimed by its supporters that by reducing wage costs BIG would create jobs. But even if it did create jobs it would do so in an indiscriminate and unplanned way. BIG would prevent employment planning. The employer who set up an armaments factory would get the same wage subsidy as a group of parents setting up a nursery. Under a minimum wage system, it would be possible to use a large part of the money (that would otherwise go on payment of BIG to all those in work) on selective subsidies to those jobs which met collectively determined needs for employment and for services. BIG responds to the problems of selectivity in income maintenance (see Chapter 2) by abandoning selectivity altogether. We think that socialism rightly proposes a quite different type of selectivity: selectivity in the development of employment and services to meet needs.

It is also important to consider the relations of power which would result from the two approaches. A minimum wage would embody the principle of a worker's right to a decent income from their employers. It would allow two vital questions to be treated separately, even if economically they prove to be closely linked: firstly, what is a reasonable minimum wage level; secondly, what subsidies are needed to maintain employment? Certainly employers would campaign against increases in the minimum wage, but those who said they couldn't afford the minimum could be pointed to the system of subsidies supporting selected industries and forms of employment. When it came to the subsidies, employers would be supplicants asking for help; they would have to bear some of the burden of selectivity that currently falls on individuals.

The likely impact of BIG on these power relations between employers and workers would be in the opposite direction. Low-paid workers and the unemployed would be the ones in the supplicant position, asking for an increase in what would be seen as a 'state hand-out'. They would be divided from better-paid workers, because BIG would make up a major part of their incomes. They would have no come-back against their own employers in this debate because the wage subsidy would be an indiscriminate one. They would be dependant on 'state generosity' in raising the BIG level.

It is argued by the proponents of BIG that it would automatically reduce or eliminate the divisions between the employed and the unemployed, but this is not so. These divisions rest on inequalities of income, and tackling such inequalities means redistributing income from the employed to the unemployed. If the scheme was to bring about the necessary redistribution, then that would have to be paid for by the higher-paid workers; undoubtedly that would lead to pressure to reintroduce means-testing, a move to which BIG lends itself (see Chapter 8). The arguments for this redistribution have to be won; that is a challenge which faces our approach as much as any other. It is misleading to suggest that the problems can be made to disappear magically by a technical change to the structure of income maintenance. The problems posed by redistribution are inescapably political.

Our Proposals

The twin problems of low pay and unemployment currently affect over 13 million adults in Britain — that is, two in five of all adults of working age. Workers and the unemployed need not be subjected to the means test and poverty, nor should reform evade the question of the responsibility of employers to pay decent wages. Our proposals are as follows:

(1) A statutory minimum wage should be introduced, applicable to part-timers at an equivalent hourly rate, to be enforced by a strengthened inspectorate.

(2) Unemployed people should be entitled to a positional benefit on an individual basis (irrespective of family circumstances), without contribution or means tests.

(3) Part-time workers should also be able to claim benefit for those hours when they are unable to find employment (as well as receiving at least the minimum wage hourly rate when working).

(4) Trade unions should have the right to enter workplaces to discuss pay, conditions and recruitment with workers, and workers should have the right to union recognition.

(5) Employment protection measures should be strengthened to prevent victimization.

(6) Equal pay legislation should be strengthened and measures introduced to outlaw discrimination in employment on grounds of sex, race, disability or sexual orientation.

(7) Equivalents of the (now abolished) Fair Wages Resolution and Schedule 11 should be introduced to compel employers to pay nationally agreed rates of pay.

Implicit in the idea of 'unemployment' is some kind of test of willingness to participate in the labour market. It would have to be a condition of receiving benefit that the individual was willing to work should a suitable job be available. We make the case for this principle in Chapter 2. A socialist approach to this question is distinguished by the acknowledgement that there is a reciprocal social responsibility to plan work and services to meet needs. This means that the state must be seen as having a responsibility to provide work, and that where this is not possible for whatever reasons the state must abandon the present policy of punishing the unemployed through the benefits system. This means that benefit must be paid at an adequate level. We think the aim should be to bring it up to the level of the minimum wage. This principle applies equally to situations in which unemployed people can only find part-time work. The income maintenance system should encourage them to take such work and should provide income support to cover those hours of the week when they are not working.

One of the criticisms often made of statutory minimum wages is the difficulty of enforcement. Enforcement is only a problem as long as there are people willing to accept low wages. At present there is a large pool of such people, because of the low level of benefits and the fact that so many people are not paid benefits at all. The approach put forward in this book, by ensuring that all adults could receive adequate incomes when out of work, (or working part-time), would largely eradicate this problem. Furthermore, as the minimum would apply to everyone, it could be widely advertised and would become well known.

Devolution of control over benefits administration to the local level would also assist with enforcement. Officials involved must have the closest possible contacts with trade unionists and community organizations in order to tap local knowledge of employment. Offices should operate at local level as employment/benefit/tax centres. People would be able to go there to find jobs, to make complaints under the minimum wage law, to claim benefit and so on. These offices could also be the administrative centres for decisions on the allocation of subsidies to develop and support local employment, although obviously such decisions would have to be taken in the context of area and national planning. The aim would be to bring together in one easily accessible place the maximum knowledge about the local economy. This would facilitate enforcement of a minimum wage, job-finding and democratic involvement in vital decisions on employment matters.

Conclusions: Income Maintenance and the Economy

At present the government and employers are trying to impose flexibility on the work-force. Workers in higher-status jobs are offered security in exchange for flexibility over work practices. Other workers have flexibility imposed on them through insecurity: they must accept whatever jobs and types of work they are offered and, as soon as they are no longer needed, they are likely to be laid off.

The proposals we put forward in this chapter and throughout the book are clearly incompatible with this type of economic strategy. Our proposals would remove the obstacles which the income maintenance system currently puts in the way of part-time work and job-sharing; this would encourage the growth of these forms of employment. But at the same time they would provide security to part-time workers by guaranteeing them a decent income in or out of work. Our proposals would also undermine differentials between high- and low-status workers by imposing a minimum wage, improving flat-rate state pensions, removing tax perks for owner-occupation and private pensions, and making the tax system generally more progressive. It will be argued that because the type of egalitarian reforms we propose run counter to current assumptions about the best way of organizing the labour market, they are incompatible with any successful economic strategy.

We reject this view, but it does point to the need to relate income maintenance reforms to economic policy. The simple adoption by the left of progressive social policies is not enough. Such policies will always be abandoned if there is a perceived choice between economic growth and social justice. An integrated strategy must be based around the offering of security at an economy-wide level through adequate benefits and policies which aim for full employment, in exchange for flexibility from workers. It would also mean attacking the rigid division of labour which imposes totally routinized systems of labour on large groups of workers, so that workers receive more rewards for working than merely cash in the hand.

Our proposals offer a way of tapping the skills and initiative of people in the community who, we believe, wish to see their local economies thriving and providing jobs, production and services, and who are willing to work to achieve this. The Thatcherite philosophy is that people have no cooperative spirit and no interest in the future of their communities. Therefore those with valuable skills must be bribed and cajoled into using them efficiently. Those without such skills must be pushed around and abused to ensure that they never lose their willingness to work. We believe that if people are given a genuine chance to participate in building a strong economy to meet their needs they will take it. The bullying could stop now.

Notes

1. C. Pond and C. Winyard, *The Case for a National Minimum Wage*, Low Pay Unit Pamphlet No. 23. London 1983. This compares to 62 per cent before the Equal Pay Act was introduced.

2. *Low Pay Review*, No. 20, London, Winter 1984.

3. HMSO, *New Earnings Survey 1984*, London 1984.

4. *Low Pay Review*, No. 20.

5. *Financial Times*, 12 November 1984.

6. *Guardian*, 24 August 1983.

7. *Low Pay Review*, No. 20.

8. Department of Employment, *The Future of Wage Councils (Consultative Paper)*, London 1985.

9. Henry Neuburger, *From the Dole Queue to the Sweatshop — Minimum Wages and Government Policy*, London 1984.

10. In particular Neuburger calculates that abolition would lead to a 12.7 per cent cut in pay for those non-manual women workers covered.

11. For a discussion of the various low-pay definitions, see *Low Pay Review*, No. 20. We favour the Low Pay Unit's definition of low pay relative to median rather than mean wages. Such an approach ensures that there is no technical obstacle to the abolition of low pay.

12. See *Low Pay Review*, No. 20, and *Employment Gazette*, January 1985, vol. 93, no. 1.

13. Colin Brown, *Black and White in Britain: The Third Survey of the Policy Studies Institute*, London 1984. The survey was carried out in 1982.

14. HMSO, *New Earnings Survey 1984*, London 1984.

15. *Labour Research Bulletin*, London, July 1984.

16. *Guardian*, 7 December 1984.

17. The government has reduced the official level of unemployment in the following way. In 1982 they changed the method of measurement so that only those actually signing on at the benefit office are now considered unemployed. By changes in the benefit system they have substantially reduced the numbers of men over age sixty signing on. These two measures have reduced the figures by around 387,542. A government labour force survey in 1981 found that only 92.3 per cent of men were registered even under the old system, accounting for another 194,000. According to the same survey, only 70 per cent of women looking for work were registered, adding another 423,000 to the jobless total. Finally, government training schemes — paying allowance at or just above benefit levels — take care of around 500,000 young people.

18. Greenwich Welfare Rights Unit, *Breadline Greenwich: Welfare Rights Implications*, London 1985.

19. Figures taken from HMSO, *Social Trends 15*, London 1985. They exclude full-time students and only apply to people of working age.

20. *General Household Survey*, 1983, quoted in *Social Trends 15*.

21. See Chapter 8 for an explanation of how higher tax allowances favour those with highest incomes.

22. A. W. Dilnot, J. A. Kay and C. N. Morris, *The Reform of Social Security*, Oxford 1984.

23. *Guardian*, 30 July 1984.

24. *Guardian*, 13 November 1984.

25. C. Pond and C. Winyard, *The Case for a National Minimum Wage*.

26. *Guardian*, 16 March 1983.

4

Women, Men and Children

In this chapter we discuss relations of dependancy and responsibility within the family. As we argued in Chapter 2 these underpin one of the key principles of the present social security system. This discussion raises three major issues: the current social security system's role in contributing to the inequalities between women and men, at home and in relation to work; the inadequate support for parents involved in child-care; and inadequate financial support for children themselves.

Inequalities

The government has been obliged, by an EEC directive on equal treatment of men and women, to move towards a position of formal equality between men and women with respect to social security. Nevertheless, some of the rules of the social security system are still formally discriminatory and the administration is certainly discriminatory. These formal changes will in any case only have a limited effect in reducing discrimination in the social security system, because it indirectly discriminates against women by basing assessments on a claimant's work record and on the family unit. It discriminates between those with well-paid jobs and a sustained pattern of work and those who have neither. It also generally excludes those who have a partner who is in work. On all these criteria women are likely to be among the losers. Despite moves towards formal equality, little seems to change in practice; women still get a significantly worse deal from social security.

The major remaining example of formal discrimination in social security rules is a consequence primarily of the long transitional period during which the lower National Insurance contribution (NIC) for married women is being phased out — a process which started in 1978. Even though the option to pay reduced NIC was removed three years previously, in 1981 3 million women were still paying a reduced NIC which effectively produces no entitlement to National Insurance (NI) benefits. This will delay their entitlement to a pension until their husband retires and even then they will only get a pension at the lower, dependant's rate. When they are in work and contributing at this reduced rate, women can not claim sickness or unemployment benefit. This reduced entitlement to benefits will continue well into the next century unless contribution rules are changed.

The following examples (which are not comprehensive) illustrate the way the social security system affects women. They describe various situations in which women may find themselves and explain how the benefits system would treat them and the consequences of changes in their circumstances.

(1) *Single Woman Working Full-time.* While a woman is in work, she pays tax and NIC. She may be entitled to housing benefit (HB), but probably no other benefits. However, should she fall sick or become unemployed, the contributions she has paid would probably entitle her to short-term NI benefits. These could be topped up by supplementary benefit (SB) and HB if necessary. If she becomes pregnant, at the birth of her child she will receive a maternity grant of £25 (a sum unchanged since 1969) and maternity allowance for up to eighteen weeks. She may be able to receive unemployment benefit after her maternity allowance runs out. She also receives £6.85 per week child benefit.

(2) *Married Woman Working Full-time.* A married woman pays the same tax as a single woman, but her husband, if he works, pays less tax than a single man because he is eligible for the married man's tax allowance. Her NIC is the same, although she can pay it at a reduced rate if she was doing so before 1978. If she is made redundant, or leaves her job, she is entitled to NI benefits, so long as she had been paying full contributions. Her entitlement to SB and HB would be calculated taking into account her husband's income. If her husband is earning, this means that she is unlikely to get SB at all. The system pushes her into financial dependance on her husband.

(3) *Single Parent Not Working.* A single mother will probably be entirely dependent on SB and HB if she has not been in work recently. She receives £4.25 one-parent benefit, but both this and child benefit are deducted from her SB and make no difference to her final income. If she starts a relationship with a man, she may find that her SB is stopped, because she is thought to be 'cohabiting' and the man is considered to be supporting her.

(4) *Married Woman with Children Who Has Not Worked for over Two Years.* In this case, we assume that the woman's husband is working full-time. Her only independent source of income is child benefit of £6.85 per child. She may also be able to claim means-tested benefits such as HB, but only if her husband's income is low.

(5) *Married Woman Caring for Disabled Relative.* Again we assume that the woman's husband is working full-time. She has no independent source of income — as a married woman she can not claim invalid care allowance. She may be able to claim means-tested benefits if her husband's income is low.

(6) *Retired Woman Living on Her Own.* The woman can claim a retirement pension if she has worked for a substantial number of years or if she is widowed and her husband had a sufficient contribution record. She is likely to need to top this up with SB or HB unless she has some form of private pension. If she has recently retired, she may get an earnings-related pension under the new state scheme, but this will only be significant if she was consistently in well-paid work.[1]

Labour Market Inequalities

Any insurance-based income maintenance system would reproduce the inequalities of the labour market which currently disadvantage women. Women are more likely to have spells in which they don't work and, when they do work, they are more likely to be low paid. The effect of this in the present social security system is that women will find that they frequently don't have a sufficient contribution record to entitle them to short-term NI benefits. When they come to claim long-term benefits, such as retirement pensions, their earnings record will be so poor that they will only be eligible for a minimum pension, unless they are able to claim on the basis of their husband's contribution record.

Women not in work who are married or living with a man and are caring for children are likely to find that the 'aggregation' rule of SB prevents them from getting any income at all. The SB system does not assess benefit on an individual basis — the needs and incomes of a married couple and children are lumped together to determine entitlement. It means that a married woman won't be able to receive SB if her husband has an income above SB level. This rule excludes millions of women from benefit entitlement. Even if a couple is entitled to SB, only one person can make a claim and almost invariably this will be the man.

Once again this is not formal discrimination against women by the DHSS. The rules for selecting who should be the claimant favour the partner who has recently been in work or signing on as available for work — and men are more likely to meet these conditions. As with contributory benefits, the discrimination is based on inequality between men and women in the labour market. The aggregation rule covers all couples, married or not, and this results in the sort of intrusive investigations into women's lives that we describe later, in the section on single parents. The injustice of the aggregation rule is compounded because of the unequal distribution of incomes between men and women within the household.

We will now consider other ways in which social security fails women by providing little or no support for carers and single parents.

Caring

The burden of caring in the family falls predominantly on women: this applies to care for disabled or elderly relatives as well as for children. Women with young children consequently face an enormous workload. A recent study of child-care concluded that women with children under five, whether they have jobs or not, spend, on average, six and a quarter hours on 'essential' tasks each day, but fathers spend only three-quarters of an hour on average. This excluded housework not related to child-care. Given the heavy commitment to child-care demanded of women, mothers have generally been forced out of full-time employment (see Table 4.1).

Table 4.1
ECONOMIC ACTIVITY OF WOMEN BY AGE OF YOUNGEST CHILD (%)

Economic Activity	*Childless Women*	*Age of Youngest Child*		
		0–4	*5–10*	*11–15*
Working full-time	78	7	16	31
Working part-time	6	20	48	45
TOTAL	84	27	64	76

Source: J. Martin and C. Roberts, 'Women and Employment: A Lifetime Perspective', London 1984, reproduced in D. Piachaud, *Round About 50 Hours'*, Poverty Pamphlet No. 64, London 1981.

For many women their caring responsibilities do not end when their children have grown up. They soon begin another period of caring, this time for an adult relative. About half of married women aged between thirty-five and sixty-four give some help to elderly or infirm relatives at some time or another. At any one time, about one in five of them have a disabled person or someone over sixty-five living with them.[2] The present social security system increases this disadvantage by failing to give carers an independent income, so making them financially dependent on another adult.

Young children need to be looked after on a full-time basis. At present the social facilities for child-care are totally inadequate: there are insufficient nursery places for young children and few places with childminders for children after school hours. No local education authority provides nursery spaces for more than a fraction of its pre-school children. Few workplaces have a nursery or crèche and a recent reinterpretation of the law by the Treasury is attempting to make workplace nurseries liable to be taxed as a perk — making them comparable to executives' cars rather than workers' canteens. Social facilities for the care of the sick, elderly or disabled are similarly scarce and inadequate.

As a consequence, in the vast majority of families which can not afford to buy these services, one person will have to give up full-time work to care for the children or an adult relative. This task usually falls to women for a variety of reasons. To begin with, on average women earn less than men, so for a couple it can seem to make more immediate economic sense for the woman to give up her work and for the family to keep the man's higher earnings. Secondly, employers do not expect that men will have their work interrupted by child-care responsibilities and consequently sometimes make it even more difficult for men to take time off for this reason. The fact that it is women who bear children obviously has a strong practical effect. Once having interrupted her employment to have the child, a woman is effectively trapped at home until she can make child-care arrangements. Finally, and very significantly, the overwhelmingly predominant social expectations are that women will be carers. Despite the success of feminism in challenging these expectations to some extent, it is still widely believed that women should care for children.

The state fails to recognize the role of carers in the family and fails to give them support through the income maintenance system. There is only one benefit provided specifically for carers, invalid care allowance, and even this is denied to married women. Carers are expected to rely on another adult for financial support. Moreover there is no financial assistance given to those who want to work and therefore need to arrange care for their children or relatives in the absence of social facilities. It is assumed that care will be provided for free by women who will depend on men in their families for financial support. Thus parents inevitably lose financially: either they work and have to pay for child-care, or one of the couple has to give up full-time work, in which case they lost out through lost wages.

Because they are usually unable to work full-time, carers have to choose between part-time jobs which generally have lower pay, or not being in paid employment at all. The rigid distinctions between full-time and part-time jobs in terms of their security, status, pay and so forth ensure that child-care responsibilities trap carers in low-paid and insecure work. Tackling this issue is an essential part of providing a framework for a more equal distribution of caring between men and women. This must be as much an objective of a progressive strategy of care as is financial independence for carers. Otherwise the payment of benefit to carers would simply increase the likelihood that women would care for children and relatives at home.

Single Parents

The relationship between income maintenance and service provision confronts one-parent families with an unpalatable choice: if the parents work full-time, then their children usually have to make do with unsuitable arrangements for care and supervision (because there is so little available); if they look after their children full-time or part-time, they have to rely on inadequate benefits for support. The problems that women experience with the income maintenance system are experienced more acutely still by those single parents who are forced into caring for their children full-time. They will end up with an inadequate contribution record, they get inadequate benefit as carers, inadequate financial support for their children, and the threat of the cohabitation rule hangs over them.

The National Council for One-Parent Families estimates that there are 1 million single parents looking after a total of 1.6 million children. Nine out of ten single parents are women (for brevity, and bearing this proportion in mind, we refer to single parents as 'she' in this chapter). A higher proportion of West Indian households (18 per cent) consist of a lone parent with children than do either Asian (4 per cent) or white households (3 per cent). Looked at another way, 31 per cent of all West Indian households with any children are headed by a lone parent compared to 5 per cent of Asian households and 10 per cent of white households.[3] Moreover these snapshot figures obscure the full extent of lone-parenthood. A higher proportion of children experience a period of living with only one parent at some time in their lives than there are children in single-parent families at any one time.[4]

Single women with children face the same difficulties in relation to jobs and pay as other women with children, but, crucially, they face the additional problem that there are never any wages coming into the household from a partner. As a consequence, whereas 95 per cent of all two-parent families rely primarily on earnings for their income, only 44 per cent of women single parents have earnings as their main source of income and about half rely predominantly on social security.[5] The only social security benefit paid exclusively to single parents is one-parent benefit of £4.25 per week. There are 441,000 single parents making do on sb.

Despite some elements of flexibility in the social security system, single parents usually have a choice between total reliance on benefits or supporting themselves exclusively through wages. We have discussed the enormous problems of people on sb trying to do part-time work. The earnings rule for sb, even though it is slightly more generous for single parents than others, nevertheless reduces benefit by £1 for each £1 increase in take-home pay above £20 per week. Apart from the hassle of working part-time and claiming benefit, the sb rules concerning payment of the long-term rate ensure that it is in a single parent's interest never to earn more than her sb entitlement, unless she is confident that the increase in her income will be sustained for many years. A parent who is off sb for more than eight weeks loses her entitlement to the long-term rate (worth £7.65 per week) for a whole year.[6] A single parent at work has to make and pay for child-care arrangements. As a result of all these complications and restrictions, a single parent has little incentive to work unless it is full-time and/or unusually well paid: 20 per cent of single mothers work full-time, whereas only 14 per cent of married mothers are full-time workers.[7]

Single parents on sb pay a very high price in lost privacy. The DHSS will attempt to discover who the children's father is and whether he is able to pay maintenance — that is, if he is in their terms a 'liable relative'. They will also often try to coerce women to seek that maintenance from him in order to save the DHSS money, not to benefit the children or mother. This pushes the woman back into financial dependency on the man from whom she has separated. A system which has such wide scope for discretion about such personal matters leaves the door open for the indulgence of any prejudice which officials may feel, such as hostility to black single parents.

The same conclusion is true of the notorious cohabitation rule. Unmarried couples are treated in the same way as married couples if they are, in the DHSS's view, 'living together as husband and wife'. The DHSS has established a series of tests for making this judgement. The sharing of expenses, the 'stability' of the relationship, the existence of a sexual relationship and the 'public appearance' of the couple will all be taken into account. Such subjective judgements necessarily involve offensive intrusions into claimants' lives. The continued threat of having benefit cut off makes it difficult for women to have any sort of relationship with a man. When such a threat is carried out it frequently forces financial dependence on the man, although it may have been unintended, unwanted and undesirable. Single parents have also been specially 'targeted' by Specialist Claims Control teams — the roving fraud squads.

The harsh earnings rules, low pay and 'liable relative' and cohabitation tests place obstructions in the way of women single parents who wish to work or enter into any kind of friendship. They must either make a dramatic change — go to work full-time or set up joint home with a man — or stay as they are. Most women single parents and their children face the choice between poverty and dependence.

Inadequate Incomes for Children

> All of a sudden the children needed a lot of clothes. One of them lost a shoe in the market and I couldn't find it, so that was a new pair that was needed. I went to the social security to ask for clothes, but they wouldn't give me a thing. When they refused that, I sat down and cried. I don't want second-hand clothes for my kids: they've never done anything wrong that I should have to put second-hand clothes on them.[8]

The DHSS itself estimates, using figures from the 1979 Family Expenditure Survey, that nearly 1¼ million nuclear families have incomes at or below 140 per cent of their SB entitlement and that 520,000 single-parent families (more than half) have this level of income.[9] Between 1977 and 1981, according to government statistics, the number of children in Britain declined by nearly 1 million, but the number in poverty and on the margins of poverty increased by 430,000 to 3 million (28 per cent).[10]

Support for children is chronically inadequate, which explains why so much attention focuses on family poverty. We think that there are two separate issues involved. We have already discussed inequality between women and men and the costs of child-care. We now turn to the issue of inadequate financial support for children themselves. Currently, social security provides for dependant children in a variety of ways. Child benefit is paid to parents in respect of each child under sixteen or still at school. There are no contribution or means tests and child benefit is not taxable. At a rate of £6.85 per week per child it falls far short of the true cost of supporting a child. Child additions of £7.65 are only payable with NI long-term benefits such as pensions (child additions for other NI benefits were abolished altogether in November 1984). The SB scale rates for the 1.72 million children dependent on SB are ludicrously low, for example, £9.60 for those under eleven. This is particularly alarming as it is assumed that a parent has no other income to meet the costs of providing for their children. Obviously £9.60 cannot possibly cover the cost of a proper diet, adequate clothing, heating, leisure and other absolute necessities. Children dependent on such incomes are denied presents, sweets, excursions and so forth, which become unobtainable 'treats'. One survey of SB claimants revealed that over half of couples with children ran out of money 'most weeks'.[11]

It is difficult to establish precisely the costs of child support. Several surveys have shown the grossly inadequate provision for children in the SB system and from child benefit, and they illustrate that child benefit needs to increase with the age of the child. One study showed that for thirteen—fifteen-year-olds the SB rate is just over half the level required.[12]

Working families on low incomes can claim Family Income Supplement (FIS) as a means-tested addition to child benefit. However this is only payable at very low income levels. Parents with two children must have a total gross income below £100 to be eligible. Moreover as a means-tested benefit it contributes substantially to the problems of the poverty trap discussed in the previous chapter. The widely canvassed proposal to means-test child benefit would only make this problem worse. Child benefit at the moment is a vital part of the system of child support without the restrictive conditions that apply to nearly all other benefits. Rather than attacking the principle of state responsibility for child support, the aim should be to extend this principle further.

Proposals

We have identified four fundamental defects of the social security system: financial inequality between women and men; the exclusion of women in particular from any right to an independent income through the use of the family as a basis for assessment; the inadequacy of child support; and the inadequacy of incomes for carers. The fundamental objective of reform must be to deal with these defects.

Income maintenance should be based on the separate treatment of adult men and women regardless of marital status, sex or assumed dependency. This requires the abolition of the aggregation and cohabitation rules.

People challenging proposals for separate assessment tend to focus on the small issue of women who are dependent on a man's income and who are not caring for children or elderly or disabled relatives. There are very few women in this position and fewer still who are well off. The far larger number of women who care for dependants at home and at present have an inadequate income and no opportunity of getting one are ignored. Moreover, other women without employment should be treated as unemployed if they are willing to make themselves available for paid employment and therefore would be eligible for unemployment benefit.

One conventional response to proposals for separate assessment is to ask rhetorically, 'Do you mean that benefit would be paid to the wife of a millionaire?' This assumes that *nothing else changes* when benefit assessment is separated. On the contrary, in our proposals the millionaire would be taxed heavily as a single person with a large income (or wealth). Consequently it is perfectly fair that anyone he lives with should have an independent income. The central issue raised by this hypothetical example of the millionaire's wife is in fact dependancy. The argument assumes that it is normal and proper for a woman to require support from her husband — yet this enforced dependancy is precisely what needs to change. Inequality is daily recreated through the need of women to receive money from their husbands for their own living expenses: this must be challenged not only because it is central to the inequalities between women and men, but also because it keeps women poor and without the dignity of an independent income. Furthermore there is no guarantee that they will receive even the subsistence incomes that they require from their husbands, or that the husband's income will be adequate for two people.

Separate assessment would contribute to the elimination of financial inequalities between women and men. However there are many other necessary changes. The abolition of contribution tests and earnings-related benefits would break the link between inequalities in jobs and pay and the social security system. A statutory minimum wage and strengthened equal pay legislation would reduce the gap between women's and men's earnings (especially since so many of the low paid are women). The proposal for benefit to be payable to part-time workers is also essential in ensuring that women have an adequate independent income.

Child-care is a social responsibility. The principal underlying the payment of 'positional benefits' is that the state supports those who can't support themselves through earning a wage at work. This applies to pensioners, the sick and unemployed, for example, and should therefore apply equally to child-carers. Separate assessment would be more or less meaningless unless benefit was paid to carers. It would also be fairly meaningless if it wasn't possible for carers to claim benefit whilst working part-time, because many carers either have or would like to have part-time jobs; at present suitable work is often difficult to arrange.

We have not discussed maternity benefits separately in this chapter. The treatment of maternity in these proposals would follow the general principles discussed. A pregnant woman could receive a 'positional' maternity benefit immediately before the birth of her child and also during any periods of sickness in her pregnancy. Proposals for reform of maternity provision should emphasize the development of state responsibility for maternity benefit rather than the strengthening of any duty on employers to provide maternity pay. Part of the package of reform must be a substantially increased maternity grant.

So far we have only described a system of supporting carers who are not in work, by ensuring their entitlement to a positional benefit. However, many parents want to work, full-time or part-time, and it is essential that they are able to do this without a reduction in their living standards. The main emphasis should be on meeting the child-care needs of working parents, or those looking for work, through low-cost state services. A statutory duty should be placed on local authorities to provide low-cost nurseries at progressively lower ages and low-cost childminding for these parents. However such a programme, even with a determined political commitment, would take considerable time to develop and implement, and the process would inevitably develop unevenly. In the meantime the positional benefit payable to parents who stayed at home to take care of children should be matched by benefits related to the cost of child-care for those parents who want to work. Without such a cost-related child-care allowance the effect of the positional benefit for carers would be to provide a huge incentive for at least one parent to stay at home rather than seek work. This could reinforce the tendency for women to be trapped in the home as carers. Some element of control of this otherwise open-ended commitment is required — for example, payments for child-care could only be made if a child goes to a registered nursery or childminder. Payments would be a fixed weekly sum based on average nursery costs.

One way of assisting the implementation of this policy would be to lower the school starting age. At present the age at which the state assumes a responsibility for educating and caring for children is arbitrarily set at five years. By lowering the school starting age the amount of special assistance of one sort or another that parents required could be reduced.

The payment of benefit to carers and the provision of low-cost child-care services raise the question of how the extent of care performed by an individual is assessed. In principle parents caring for children at home should be able to work part-time and receive benefit for the time they are involved in care. For some people, caring for children may not be a full-time responsibility, for example, older children are at school for part of the week. Other people might choose to care for children part-time and work part-time. In either case there would be a need to assess the level of care required, for the purpose of paying benefit.

One solution would be to consider that a person looking after a child under five (the age at which children start school) is involved in full-time child-care. Those whose youngest child was of school age (presently five to sixteen years) would be entitled to a carer's benefit on, say, a half-time basis. In this case a carer would either be able to work part-time to make up their income, or, if they were unable to find work, would receive unemployment benefit for that part of the week. The net effect would be that if they were not working they would receive the same income as someone caring full-time, since both unemployment and carer's benefit would be paid at the same level. A person with a child under five who wished to work could either get low-cost child-care or a child-care allowance while they were working and carer's benefit for the time they spent at home. One advantage of this flexible system would be that where there was an entitlement to full-time carer's benefit a couple could share caring responsibilities — each getting part-time carer's benefit and working part-time.

An identical system of carer's benefits would be payable to those caring for disabled people, but in this case the assessment of the level of care needed would be related to the degree of disability.

Complementing the payment of benefit to carers, there would need to be a variety of part-time jobs available so that all parents would have the option of combining work with a high degree of involvement in the care of their own children. Indeed it would be wrong to see the necessary reforms as being wholly directed to the position of women as carers. It is essential that adequate benefits and flexible working arrangements are available to both men and women to break down the expectation that women will be responsible for caring.

The state must ensure adequate support for children. The principal that education is an essential investment in society's future is almost universally accepted. The payment of child benefit at the moment weakly follows that same principle and has strong popular support. This principle should be extended to ensure that child benefit meets the full necessary costs of child support. The current level of child benefit, £6.85, makes it little more than a token of support. Child benefit must be raised to a level equal to the full necessary cost of providing for a child (food, clothing, heating, travel, school clothes, etc.). Part of the child benefit payment representing roughly the consumption costs of a child (food, heating, etc.) for the time she/he was in a state nursery would be payable to that nursery if the parents were at work. Research indicates that child benefit needs to increase with age, so that by the age of sixteen or seventeen it would become comparable with the adult rate of benefit. Child benefit could be paid in respect of each child to the parent/adult who actually provided the care for that child. If care was shared, then parents should be able to choose to whom it was paid, otherwise, or in cases of disagreement, women should have priority over men, as should natural parents over other adults.

Let us look at some practical consequences of these proposals:

(1) *Single Woman Working Full-time.* While in work a single woman would be guaranteed a minimum wage and equal pay with male employees. She would pay tax but no separate NIC. Should she fall sick or become unemployed, she would be entitled to positional benefits at a standard rate without tests of contributions or means. Should she decide to have a child she would be entitled to the same level of positional benefit from the time she has to give up work. On the birth of her child she would receive a maternity grant and child benefit; she would continue to receive benefit as a full-time carer until such time as she might choose to return to work.

(2) *Married Woman Working Full-time.* A married woman would pay tax, assessed on the same basis as a single woman, and would have the same pay and

employments rights and have the same entitlement to positional benefits in case of unemployment, sickness or pregnancy. Neither the assessment of her taxes nor her benefits would be affected by her marriage or her husband's income.

Should she have a child under school age, she or her husband would receive child benefit. They would have a number of options regarding care. For example, one of them could choose not to work nor to look for work and could claim carer's benefit on a full-time basis. Secondly, both of them could choose to work or be available for work part-time — both claiming carer's benefit on a part-time basis. Thirdly, both of them could choose to work or look for work and forgo their right to carer's benefit. The state would then be obliged to provide low-cost child-care or, if this was not possible, pay child-care cost allowance.

(3) *Single Parent Not Working.* If the youngest child was under school age the single parent would receive carer's benefit on a full-time basis and child benefit free from the threat of the cohabitation rule. When the youngest child reached school age s/he would have to be willing to accept part-time work, and would therefore get a combination of carer's benefit and unemployment benefit (paid at identical rates) or of carer's benefit and a wage.

(4) *Married Woman Caring for a Disabled Relative.* Regardless of whether the woman's husband works, she would receive carer's benefit depending only on the level of care required by the disabled person. Alternatively, her husband could provide the care and receive benefit.

(5) *Retired Woman Living on Her Own.* She would receive a pension in her own right at a flat rate free of contribution or means tests. We discuss pensions in detail in the next chapter.

Notes

1. The social security system gives preferential treatment to widows. Relative to other national insurance benefits, widows' benefits are generous: there is no earnings rule, they are paid at the highest rate and have relatively lenient contribution tests. Widow's allowance is paid for twenty-six weeks after the death of a husband; widowed mother's allowance is paid after that period if the woman has children; and widow's pension is payable if widowhood begins or parental responsibility ends after she is forty. The relative generosity of widow's benefits is such that in the December 1982 annual statistical survey the DHSS found only 6,000 of the 75,000 women claiming widowed mother's allowance were also claiming SB.

2. Mary McIntosh, *The Welfare State and the Needs of the Dependent Family*, in: ed, *Fit Work for Women*, Oxford 1981

3. Colin Brown, *Black and White in Britain: The Third Survey of the Policy Studies Institute*, London 1984.

4. A survey undertaken by the University of Bristol (reported in National Consumer Council 1984 *Of Benefit to All*,) discovered that by the age of five, 11 per cent of children in the study had experienced a period of being in a one-parent family, although only 6 per cent were in a one-parent family at that age.

5. Eighty per cent of all single fathers rely primarily on earnings.

6. Single parents on SB are not expected to sign on as available for work and are therefore entitled to the long-term rate after one year.

7. *General Household Survey*, London 1982, Table 6.104.

8. 'Terry' speaking about life on SB, quoted in Paul Harrison, *Inside the Inner City*, London 1983.

9. *Social Security Statistics*, 1983, Table 47.07.

10. Peter Townsend, *Fewer Children, More Poverty*, Bristol 1984, Table 2.

11. Policy Studies Institute, *Study of the 1980 Reform of Supplementary Benefits*, London, 1984, Table A24.

12. D. Piachaud, *Round About 50 Hours a Week*, Poverty Pamphlet No. 64, London 1981.

5
Pensions

In 1984, the market value of occupational pension funds was estimated to be £150 thousand million and they were growing at the rate of £13.50 thousand million every year.[1] For the state's part, it spent around £15.35 thousand million on pensions for the elderly in 1983/4 — 46.5 per cent of all spending on benefits — and tax exemptions for private pensions total £5.1 thousand million.[2] In addition the special tax allowance for the elderly, the age allowance, costs £500 million.[3] Pensions are large-scale business — for the City and for the state. Sums are done in thousand millions — you can lose count of the noughts. But pensions are also calculated in pounds and pence. Most pensioners can't afford to lose 10p — let alone a few noughts — in the weekly equation they do, trying to balance their weekly budget. And often the sums simply don't add up. More than 3 million pensioners live at or below the supplementary benefit level, trying to stretch £35.70 to cover their food, clothing, heating, leisure and all other items of 'normal' expenditure. How can it be that a pensions industry with a turnover running into billions of pounds of private money, including large amounts of state subsidy and accompanied by a large direct state expenditure, can fail to keep pensioners from poverty? In this chapter we consider the present provision for pensioners, the plans of the two main parties for development of pensions in the future, and propose an approach more likely to meet the real needs of pensioners.

Pensions Now

The system of state pensions currently in force conforms to the 'binary principle' we described in Chapter 1, with all the attendant problems that that implies. The current rate of contributory retirement pension for a single pensioner is £35.80 — just 10p higher than the corresponding supplementary benefit (SB) rate. A couple on retirement pension get £57.30, compared to £57.10 on SB. The result of the low rate of the non-means-tested retirement pension is that a huge number of pensioners have to claim means-tested benefits of one sort or another. At the end of 1983 there were 9,285,000 people getting retirement pension:[4] its inadequacy is shown by the fact that 1,698,000 of these pensioners have to claim SB,[5] and in 1984 3.65 million pensioners were getting means-tested housing benefit (HB).[6]

Since 1978 the state earnings-related pension scheme (SERPS) has been in operation:

How Does SERPS Work?

There are two elements to pensions paid under SERPS: the basic pension and the earnings-related component. The introduction of SERPS was accompanied by a new system of contributions which determines entitlement to the basic pension. Contributors who earn more than the 'lower earnings limit' (£35.50 in 1985/6) pay a variable proportion of their earnings in National Insurance contributions. Some of those who are not working — such as the unemployed and sick — can be 'credited' with contributions which protect their entitlement to the basic pension. Contributors are allowed to have gaps in their contribution records equivalent to about one year in every ten of their working lives without their basic pension being affected. If the 'gaps' (years with insufficient credits or contributions) amount to more than this they receive a reduced basic pension.

The earnings-related element is paid at a low level to a minority of pensioners now, but would become an increasingly important feature over the next thirty years. It is worked out like this. Earnings for each year since the scheme started in 1978 are indexed for inflation. At retirement, the twenty years in which the person has earned most are selected. The average of these twenty 'best years' is worked out and a sum equal to the lower earnings limit is knocked off (£35.50 in 1985/6). If the average is higher than the upper earnings limit (currently £265), the excess is also ignored. The earnings-related payment is a quarter of what is left. It is uprated annually in the same way as the basic pension — that is, at the moment, in line with price increases.

The deduction of the lower earnings limit from the average earnings results in a disproportionately high earnings-related payment to those on higher earnings. Someone who has had average earnings of £80 a week will be treated as having averaged £45.50 — just over half the true figure. On the other hand, someone who has earned an average of £200 is treated as having averaged £164.50 — over three-quarters of the real figure.

If the claimant doesn't have twenty years' earnings since 1978, the earnings-related payment is reduced proportionately, so no one would get a full payment until the first people retire in 1998, and even then they will need to have been in continuous employment since 1978.

Under SERPS those women who have adequate contribution records can get pensions at the appropriate single person's rate, so there is a form of separate assessment in state pensions. But this only applies to those married women who have worked in the past and have had sufficient earnings to contribute (many part-time women workers earn less than the lower earnings limit of £35.50 and so do not contribute at all). Around two-thirds of those getting retirement pension at the moment are women, but, of these 6 million women, around 4 million have to rely on their husbands' contributions to get pensions. Over 2 million of these women are widows and they get the retirement pension at the same rate their husbands would have got as single pensioners. But women who are neither widowed nor separated are effectively treated as 'dependants', getting retirement pension at a reduced rate of £21.50 (compared to £35.80). Moreover when it comes to claiming SB and HB, separate assessment is right out: the couple's income and needs are assessed together. There seems to have been a growing recognition in the social security and taxation systems that separate assessment is in practice justified: but it is treated as too good for those on the lowest incomes.

In addition to the basic retirement pension, there are various additions payable. SERPS has been described above. Pensioners can also receive 'graduated pension' based on earnings-related contributions to the scheme introduced in 1959, but these are not indexed for inflation and are usually very small. They also get the princely sum of 25p a week once they reach the age of eighty. Pensioners can also earn extra pension by deferring retirement: those who do not give up work at pensionable age (sixty-five for men, sixty for women) get an increased pension when they do retire, or after five years. Those who retire at pensionable age are subject to the 'earnings rule': if they go back to work (for instance, part-time) and earn above £70 a week, they lose all or part of their pension. There has been considerable discussion about equalizing pensionable ages. In a sense this has been achieved in the SB scheme, but only as a result of the government's desire to limit the unemployment figures: unemployed men over the age of sixty can receive the same rate of SB payable to pensioners, but only on condition that they do not sign on as unemployed.

Given the low rate of the basic pension, the only way most pensioners can avoid reliance on means-tested benefits is through getting a private pension, usually from an occupational scheme set up by their previous employers. Despite the huge size and rate of growth of these schemes, only around a third of pensioners get private pensions, and the amount paid out is around £5 thousand million a year — under a third of the cost of the state scheme.[7] This relationship is due to be reversed over the next fifty years, with benefits paid out by private schemes projected to rise to £30 billion a year by 2024.[8] We discuss the implications of this transformation of the relationship between the state and private sectors below.

The basic pension is glaringly inadequate by international standards. In 1984, at 19.2 per cent of gross average earnings, the single person's pension was lower than in any other EEC country and was less than half the level of the pensions paid in Germany and France.[9] While this situation continues, pensioners will be divided into those who can top up their basic pension by some form of earnings-related pension and those (currently over a third of all pensioners) who are forced on to some form of means-tested benefit. Yet the current political debate on pensions focuses on the way in which earnings-related pensions should be provided — that is, the balance between state and private provision — rather than on the level of the basic pension itself. The rest of this chapter examines the background to the debate between state and private provision. But, more fundamentally, it questions the assumption that earnings-related pensions are an effective way to guarantee adequate incomes in old age.

State Pension Plans

The introduction of SERPS in 1975 ended a period of nearly two decades in which the future of pensions had been politically contested. The Labour Party decided to attempt to de-politicize the issue by putting forward a plan in which the state would have a major role but which also offered substantial encouragement to the private sector, and agreement was reached with the Conservatives on the plan. The advantages of such a bi-partisan approach were thought to be that the future of pensions would be assured, irrespective of the electoral fortunes of Labour. The plan involved increasing state expenditure on pensions substantially over the following half century. SERPS would also provide substantially better pensions for those in regular employment and on near to average earnings.

In 1979 the in-coming Conservative government seemed to share the objectives of SERPS and to this extent the bi-partisan approach appeared to be paying dividends. The government declared its 'firm intention that pensioners and other long-term beneficiaries can confidently look forward to sharing in the increased standards of living of the country as a whole'.[10] Unfortunately, actions speak louder than words. SERPS included a commitment to raising the basic pension in line with wages or prices, whichever was the higher. In other words, the basic pension was at least pegged to a more or less constant share of national income. The first thing the new government did in relation to pensions was to cut this link.[11] As a result of this cut it has been calculated that the value of the pension will fall by more than half over a forty-year period — that is, by the time today's thirty-five-year-olds are seventy-five.[12] They then turned their attention to the earnings-related component of SERPS. During Cabinet discussions of the review of pensions set up by Norman Fowler, they have let it be known that they consider the projected increase in state expenditure on SERPS to be unacceptably high and have declared their intention of phasing out the earnings-related element of SERPS in favour of private provision. The Conservative approach to pensions is much as you would expect: to ignore the question of need among the elderly and focus attention on means of cutting public spending on pensions through privatization.

A natural response to the Tory onslaught is to defend SERPS unquestioningly. SERPS does promise some gains — an increase in state expenditure on pensions and the reduction in the extent of poverty among the elderly. But we need to question whether SERPS itself meets socialist objectives. That means not resting with general questions concerning the level of pensions expenditure and the balance between state and private provision, but also getting down to specifics: who would get what from SERPS, and when?

One consequence of the plan to introduce SERPS in a very gradual way is that during the long introductory period there would be large inequalities between young and old pensioners. Even at the turn of the century there would be large numbers of pensioners who had retired before April 1979 and would get nothing at all from the scheme. For example, it has been calculated that in the year 2001, women over the age of eighty would on average be getting pensions at two-thirds the level being paid to women aged between sixty and sixty-four.[13] For similar reasons the long-term unemployed face a bleak future under SERPS; the effect here would be particularly vicious for those made redundant in their forties or fifties during the phasing in of the new scheme. The years of work prior to 1978 would simply be ignored and such a worker could end up reaching pensionable age in 1990 or 1995 — when SERPS would theoretically be coming 'on stream' — and yet find that their earnings-related pension is derisory. Because of the low level of the basic pension they would face a bleak retirement on SB.

This is a 'temporary problem' — for the state, if not for those who experience it. The even more shocking inequalities among wage-earners are a permanent feature of the scheme. Consider three men, all with full pension records. Let us call them Mr Manual, Mr Average and Mr Manager. Mr Manual earned half average earnings; he retired in 1983, getting a state pension of £36.03. Mr Average earned average wages and retired at the same time; his state pension is £41.05. Mr Manager earned 1.5 times average earnings and his state pension is £44.76 (doubtless topped up by a lucrative private pension). Their daughters, by coincidence, will all be retiring in 1998 and will have earned at the same levels as their fathers. They will benefit in full from SERPS. Ms Manual will get £45.56, around 26.5 per cent better than her father. She will probably still have to claim SB — at any rate her income will be very close to that level after paying housing costs. Ms Average will get £65.65 — a 60 per cent improvement on what her father got. She shouldn't have to claim SB, but whether she is much above that level will depend on other factors such as housing costs. Ms Manager is the one who really does better than her dad. She gets £80.48, an 80 per cent improvement. So the benefits are 26.5 per cent, 60 per cent, 80 per cent: this is redistribution but in the wrong direction.[14]

The position of women in relation to the basic retirement pension was improved by the introduction of SERPS. Entitlement to the basic pension is preserved during up to twenty years spent caring for children or a disabled person by Home Responsibilities Protection (HRP). It is no longer possible for married women to opt to pay a reduced contribution (the 'married women's stamp') and so forfeit their pension rights. Although SERPS has improved the position of women, it has by no means abolished discrimination. People — most often women — who look after children and subsequently care for a disabled person as well can exhaust the twenty years' protection HRP provides for their basic pension entitlement. Those women who were paying reduced contributions prior to 1978 can continue to do so — and in April 1981 nearly 3 million women were still paying these contributions, which leave women with reduced pension rights.

Since the earnings-related component of SERPS is based on earnings above the lower earnings limit, the low paid — especially women in part-time work — are likely to have to continue to rely primarily on the basic pension. Black people are also likely to find themselves at the lower end of the widening range of pensions. As we saw in Chapter 3, they tend to be concentrated in the lowest-paying jobs, a cardinal sin as far as SERPS is concerned. Those who have entered Britain during the course of their working lives have the added problem that their basic pension is likely to be cut as a result of the years when they were living abroad and not contributing. Indeed anyone whose employment is interrupted, whether by unemployment, care responsibilities, disablity or for any other reason, suffers under SERPS.

Many people respond to this type of argument by saying, 'Ah, but the new scheme is contributory.' The contributory principle (which we criticized in Chapter 2) has a particularly important role in relation to pensions. Many people believe that private pensions can provide security in old age because they save and invest contributors' money. It is also believed that the state scheme is and should be modelled on this idea of a 'pension fund'. These beliefs are mythical, particularly in relation to state pensions. The state scheme is a 'pay-as-you-go' scheme. In other words contributions are not 'saved' or 'invested' in order to pay for future pensions and benefits. They are simply transferred, immediately, into the pockets of today's pensioners and claimants. Contributions are like any other form of taxation, except that they are even more regressive and are linked arbitrarily to benefit entitlements. Contributions are not set at a level to pay for future benefits, they are only set at a sufficient level to pay for benefits being paid to pensioners now.

As with so many of the welfare reforms produced by the social democratic consensus of the post-war years, SERPS is a scheme conceived of in terms of averages and stereotyped notions of careers and work patterns. By operating in this manner it serves to undermine the political case for state pensions. Aping the private sector, it perpetuates the myth that the contributory principle is the safest and fairest way of guaranteeing pensions in the future. Moreover, by adopting the same rules and assumptions as private sector pensions, it ignores the needs of those same groups — women, the low paid, the unemployed, the disabled, black people — who are least likely to be covered by private schemes. Rather than posing as a clear alternative exposing the failings of private sector provision, SERPS simply appears as a pale imitation of the original.

A Partnership for the Future?

Private pension funds at the moment appear to be one big success story. Wielding enormous economic power, growing at an extraordinary rate, they claim to provide the only route to a comfortable old age. But the very rate at which private pension funds are growing makes this success highly suspect. At the moment the contributors to occupational funds outnumber the beneficiaries by more than three to one, but when the current generation of workers retires that will no longer be the case: no one can really tell how successful the private schemes will seem then. Moreover the apparent success of the funds is heavily dependent on a government guarantee and on substantial subsidies to back it up. The Tory emphasis on expanding private provision — and indeed their arguments in favour of privatizing SERPS altogether — rests on a fallacy: the idea that private pension schemes are 'self-sufficient'.

Under the pensions scheme introduced in 1978, occupational pension funds are given a choice. They can contract themselves (and the employees concerned) out of SERPS: the employees will still be eligible for the basic state retirement pension, but won't get any state earnings-related pension. Or they can leave the employees in SERPS and simply top up the state system with a private one. In 1979 11.8 million employees were covered by occupational pension schemes, just over half the work-force. Of these, 10.3 million (87 per cent) were 'contracted out'.[15] In exchange for contracting out of the state scheme the funds receive a rebate on National Insurance contributions equal to 6.25 per cent of the earnings of each employee covered.

You might think that in exchange for this rebate, the 'contracted-out' scheme would undertake to guarantee to pay at least the pension that the beneficiary would have received under SERPS: not so. In fact all the funds must do is promise to pay a 'guaranteed minimum pension' (GMP) in addition to the basic state pension. The GMP differs from an entitlement to earnings-related pension under SERPS in several crucial respects. The GMP need only be based on average (re-valued) lifetime earnings, rather than on the best twenty years' earnings as with SERPS. Even more remarkably, the GMP is not indexed after retirement. The state guarantees to make up the difference between the GMP and the earnings-related component of SERPS — a guarantee which will get more and more expensive as years of retirement go on and the value of the GMP is undermined by inflation. Moreover, the state undertakes to make up the difference between the 'notional' GMP and the SERPS entitlement even if in fact the actual private pension exceeds both figures. The funds can contract to pay whatever level of pension they can afford, in the full knowledge that the state will treat them as having been able to afford only the 'minimum' — and that minimum is calculated in such a way as to fall steadily in real value.

This is not the only subsidy that the state provides to private pension schemes: let's consider the tax treatment of the various activities of pension funds. An employee who is 'contracted in' to the state scheme pays their NI contributions out of taxed income. The employee who is contracted out, by contrast, pays 6.85 per cent in NI and any contribution above that sum made by him/her or by the employer is tax exempt.[16] Each £1 which the fund receives only costs the employee 70p, if s/he is a basic rate tax payer, and less if s/he is a higher rate taxpayer. The state makes up the difference. The next tax concession is that both the capital gains and investment income of pension funds are untaxed. Finally, part of the pension itself can be paid as a tax-free lump sum, as long as the amount does not exceed 1.5 times the employee's final salary. So an executive earning £40,000 a year at retirement could receive a tax-free golden handshake of £60,000. Payments made in this way have not been subject to tax at any stage of the process: not when the contributions were first earned and paid over to the fund; not when they then appreciated in value and earned interest; and not when they are paid back to the now retiring member.[17] For technical reasons, it is difficult to determine exactly how much extra tax revenue would be raised by withdrawing any or all of these exemptions, but the current cost of each of them is estimated as follows: private pension contributions, £2.59 thousand million; pension fund investment income, £2.25 thousand million; lump-sum pension payments, £0.65 thousand million.[18] If unchecked, the cost of these exemptions would rise massively over the next few decades as pension funds continue to grow.

The character of occupational pension funds is such that (like SERPS) they reinforce all the inequalities in the labour market that we identified in Chapter 3. Only around a half of all employees are covered by occupational pension schemes and there are over 2.5 men covered for every one woman. In 1979 only around one in thirteen women part-time workers were in schemes. Well over a third of pension fund members are covered by schemes which distinguish between 'staff' and 'manual workers', and usually it is the manual workers who come off worse.[19] The method of calculating pensions on average lifetime earnings discriminates heavily against anyone whose employment is interrupted

— for example, by child-care responsibilities or long-term unemployment. It also discriminates against those who have only worked part of their lives in this country, in particular black first-generation immigrants. Bias against blacks in employment will also be reflected in the provision of private pensions in retirement.

In 1978, pension funds already held 16.8 per cent of all shares — and they have nearly tripled in value since then.[20] Pension fund managers control a huge proportion of the money available for investment in the national economy and they use this power irresponsibly. They have channelled vast sums of money abroad, particularly after the Tory government removed exchange controls in 1979. Financial institutions — pension funds, unit trusts, insurance companies — channelled £1.3 thousand million out of the country in just three months from July to September 1982. According to the *Guardian* the financial 'community' was 'hedging its bets against the possibility of a Labour election victory'.[21] Pension funds are often advised on investment decisions by stockbrokers who also advise the major multinational companies who are large-scale recipients of pension fund money. The City can literally run the whole show from beginning to end, for example, organizing 'dawn raids' on companies — colluding to take over control of a company.

The people who exercise such power are using employees' money, many of them trade unionists. Table 5.1 shows the major pension funds.

In 1982, Arthur Scargill, who was a trustee of the miners' pension fund, decided to refuse to accept the proposed investment plan. He argued that it was not in the miners' interest to invest abroad, or massively in the oil industry. Moreover he had consulted with the National Union of Mineworkers' membership via the annual conference and had won unanimous support for this view. But that did not ensure that the view went down any better with the non-union trustees. Arthur Scargill reported the reaction: 'You would have thought that I had dropped a bomb when I said I was not accepting it. All those people in pinstripe suits and red carnations — the shock on their faces should have been captured on camera.'[22] However the courts took an equally dim view of miners attempting to influence the investment of 'their' money. Vice-Chancellor Sir Robert Megarry, who has since been involved in several other cases involving the NUM, ruled that the possible benefits to miners of Scargill's plan were 'far too speculative and remote'.[23] Apparently the City's reasons for investing billions of pounds abroad are less 'speculative' than a plan to invest in the British economy — or so it appears to the judges. Despite the apparently absurd nature of this ruling, its implications are potentially catastrophic. What it seems to entail is that £13 thousand million or so annually of new investment money, coming largely from wage packets and salary checks plus a large government subsidy, must, according to the law, be invested according to criteria developed by the City: the interests of workers as workers cannot be taken into account. As Minns put

Table 5.1
MAJOR UK PENSION FUNDS: CAPITAL VALUE

	April 1984 £ millions
Post Office/British Telecom	6,850.0
National Coal Board	5,000.0
Electricity Supply	3,000.0
British Rail	2,550.0
British Steel	2,150.0
British Gas	2,050.0
British Petroleum	1,591.4
Airways	1,407.0
Water Authorities	824.0
Merchant Navy	806.2
UK Atomic Energy	796.1
Strathclyde Regional Council	750.0
Greater London Council	716.0
Greater Manchester Council	686.2
West Midlands County Council	680.0
British Leyland	664.5
British Aerospace	600.0
Rolls Royce	515.2
London Transport	505.2
West Yorkshire County Council	500.0
Civil Aviation Authority	454.6
Merseyside County Council	405.8
South Yorkshire County Council	312.8
National Bus	279.5
British Shipbuilders	276.0
South of Scotland Electricity	272.6
International Computers Limited	232.5
British Airports	154.4
Cable and Wireless	153.9
Northern Ireland Electricity	112.0
British Sugar	89.0

Source: Richard Minns, *Marxism Today*, London, August 1984

it, even before this ruling, 'Because of the overseas orientation of UK finance, our savings are . . . used against us. Industry is multinational, finance is multinational, but the workforce is *here*.'[24]

The government is in any case faced by serious difficulties in its plans to privatize state pensions. The first set of problems relates to the treatment of those who have already paid contributions for a state earnings-related pension payment. It would be politically very unpopular not to honour those contributions by at least freezing SERPS entitlements already earned. This also means continuing SERPS payments to those pensioners already receiving them. But such a policy would not save the government any money on its current pensions bill. It would also leave the problem of what to do with those workers currently expecting that SERPS will provide them with an adequate pension by the time they retire. The government's answer to that problem seems to be to push these workers into private pension schemes.

In turn that solution would create a second set of problems for the government, related to the cost of such a privatization plan to the state. It would entail a massive growth in the already large state subsidies to the private sector through tax exemptions. The cost of the state undertaking to top up private pensions to the level the contributor would have earned from SERPS would also grow enormously. It would be anomalous to continue this subsidy once SERPS had gone, but its withdrawal would undermine the private schemes which the government aims to strengthen.

Finally, the abolition of SERPS in favour of private provision would increase the immediate costs of pensions borne by today's workers. The same level of National Insurance contributions (NIC) would be required from them to finance today's pensions, because the state scheme operates on a 'pay-as-you-go' basis. But in addition they would have to pay private contributions to fund their own future pensions. So privatizing SERPS now would effectively mean asking today's workers to pay more to get much the same in retirement.

The government's dilemma is summed up in the question of the NIC rebate currently paid to those workers in occupational pension schemes 'contracted out' of SERPS. If SERPS goes, then logically the rebate should be extended to all those currently covered by SERPS, but this would reduce government revenue considerably. On the other hand, abolishing the rebate would mean saying to those currently in private schemes that the abolition of the state scheme requires them to contribute more to the state's NI fund. In essence the privatization of state earnings-related pensions would mean asking workers to take a cut in their living standards in exchange for pension entitlements which they have already been promised.

The government would doubtless justify the change on the grounds that previous promises of pensions have been irresponsible. They would argue that the shift from public to private provision is necessary to put the nation's pensions policy on a 'sound financial footing'. In debates on pensions policy the government hopes to exploit the faith many people place in private pensions and the justifiable mistrusts that people feel of politically vulnerable state pensions. Yet this distinction is in a fundamental sense misguided: private pensions are not in some absolute sense 'secure'. We have seen that they receive substantial subsidies from the state in the form of NI rebates and tax exemptions: these subsidies are the result of political decisions. But in a more general sense the pensions which they are able to pay will always be conditioned by political decision on the distribution of incomes: this is so despite the fact that private pensions rely on the investment of contributions. Even with a low level of inflation the value of pensions is highly dependant on the degree to which they are indexed. But pensions can only be fully indexed on the basis of a state guarantee, and that state guarantee always depends on a commitment to meet any shortfall (between contributions collected and index-linked benefits to be paid out) on a 'pay-as-you-go' basis.[25] In every sense the 'success story' of the private pension funds is dependant on the political support they receive.

Out of the Pensions Morass

In the lead up to the 1983 election, *The Times* took great pleasure in reporting a 'split' in the Labour leadership over pensions policy. The leader of the party, Michael Foot, wanted to commit a future Labour government at least to restoring the cuts made by the Tory government in the real value of the pension. Peter Shore, on the other hand, acting as shadow Chancellor of the Exchequer, implied that this was 'too costly' and presented figures to the press to prove it. According to Shore, a Labour government would 'start to make good' the cuts, quite different from a pledge to restore them in full.[26]

The disagreement exposed the extent to which Labour had been pushed into a defensive posture on pensions policy — arguing over the extent to which Tory cuts should be restored, rather than formulating a plan for improved provision. As the Tory attack on the bi-partisan policy of the 1970s has gathered pace — first, reneging on the agreement to uprate basic pensions in line with earnings and, secondly, mounting an attack on the earnings-related component of SERPS — the Labour response has been simply to defend that bi-partisan policy uncritically. In an attempt to resist Tory cuts there is a grave danger of the Labour Party making firm commitments to a policy which can't be justified on its own merits. Yet the weakness of the Tory approach lies in the increased costs which the privatization of pensions would impose on today's workers and in the way that privatization would intensify inequalities: it does not lie in the intrinsic merit of SERPS itself. In our view, the principle embodied in SERPS of increased state expenditure on pensions should be defended, as should the original commitment at least to raise the basic pension in line with earnings. But the inegalitarianism of the earnings-related component of SERPS demands a critical response. The left should be distancing itself from that element of the scheme, in favour of increased basic pensions.

One alternative response to the Tory attacks on SERPS would be to propose committing the planned growth in state expenditure to increases in the basic pension. It would be necessary to preserve existing pension rights — but the balance of projected new expenditure on earnings-related pensions could be channelled into the basic pension. Such a policy would ensure that the pension level steadily increased relative to average earnings — and that all pensioners derived the benefits, not just those younger ones with SERPS contributions. In addition to this commitment, a substantial immediate increase in the basic pension would be needed.

Not only should the basic pensions be raised, but it should be non-contributory. As we argued in Chapter 2, the purpose of contribution tests is to exclude some claimants from benefits which are reckoned necessary for others, and their effects are to reproduce inequality and hardship. Pensions provide the strongest basis for the support for the contribution principle, in both private and state schemes. If many people believe in the 'contributory principle', it is at least in part because no one has bothered to inform them that it doesn't actually work. It's a convenient con: both for the government which thereby justifies a major tax, calls it by another name and legitimates the exclusion from benefits of many in need; and for liberals who fear that people will only support social welfare on the basis of a deception. The left should start focusing attention on those who lose from the contribution system.

We are of course in favour of separate assessment in pensions. The abolition of contributions would lead naturally to the extension of separate assessment — at present restricted to those women who contribute in their own right to state or private schemes — to all women regardless of their work record. In our view there should be one age at which men and women receive a pension and there should be no reduction of the pension in respect of earnings or any other income, although both pensions and other income should be taxable. It seems to us that at the moment — with life expectancy having increased substantially — that sixty-five may be the appropriate pensionable age. If the pensionable age of women was to be raised it would have to be done on a gradualist basis so as not to disappoint the expectations of older women who actually plan and wish to retire at sixty. There is also an argument for lower retirement ages for workers in manual occupations, both because they are likely to have started work earlier and because of the damaging impact of manual work on health, leading to shorter life expectancy. But we think it would be a more positive solution not simply to 'pension off' cleaners, machinists or builders at sixty or fifty-five, but to look at ways in which at a certain age workers could be given the opportunity to transfer to other less physically demanding types of work. Such workers could, for example, be involved in education, training, social services or child-care. This approach would break down both the sexual division of labour and the restriction of some workers to unhealthy employment; moreover it would provide a much easier transition from the world of full-time work to that of retirement.

Unemployment in our society involves two fundamental problems for most people — these are extreme poverty and a sense of a 'wasted life' (through isolation, lack of purpose, a feeling of not being able to contribute to society, etc.). In slightly different forms both these problems persist in retirement. Pensions are higher than benefits paid to the unemployed, but most pensioners have to plan to live off them for the rest of their lives without even the possibility of a job to top up their savings or pay off their debts. We do not think society should throw the skills and commitment of either the unemployed or pensioners on to the scrap heap. And it is not a solution to either problem — as leading members of the main parties seem to believe — to rename the 'unemployed' as 'pensioners'. Therefore pensionable age should be an age at which you can rely on a definite income and can work as much or as little as you feel is appropriate.

Finally, we need to turn our attention to private pensions. It may seem to many that there is no room for such institutions as pension funds in a socialist approach. We agree, but the answer may be to transform them through radical reform, rather than to attempt the difficult task of abolishing them altogether. We assume that in the foreseeable future, socialist or otherwise, there will be forms of private saving. Pension funds could be just one form of such saving, meeting a particular requirement: if you like, the desire to defer some income to be consumed in old age. There is no justification for state subsidy to private pensions, particularly not in the form of tax allowances which favour the rich rather than the poor and whose quantity is controlled by the recipients of the subsidy through the scale of their operation, rather than by the giver, that is, the state. This means bringing the taxation of private pensions into line with other forms of saving (see Chapter 8). Pension funds should be regulated and monitored to ensure that they promote rather than hinder equality. Those employers who provide occupational pension funds for a substantial proportion of their employees should be required to offer the facility to all their staff (barring obvious exceptions such as those working for very short periods). The pensions of those who leave their jobs should be protected to the same degree as those who stay. Funds should be compelled to offer the same benefits to manual workers and white-collar staff.

After the legal decision concerning the mineworkers' pension fund there is an even more compelling case for legislation regarding the investment of these huge sums of money. At the very minimum, employee representation on boards of trustees should be compulsory and the funds should be required to make investment decisions bearing the long-term interests of the employees regarding employment, the economy, etc., in mind, as well as considerations of short-term 'return' on investment. But it seems that the only way of countering the power of City institutions over the funds is likely to be to syphon off a portion of the funds into forms of social investment through national investment banks or through enterprise boards. Some local authorities have already looked at the use of some of their funds in this way. Ultimately it may be that nationalization of the funds is the only way to bring them under social control, but there are many measures which can be taken which are easier to achieve.

The measures we have proposed are extremely simple, but they imply a radical change of direction. At the moment we are faced with a choice between the unfettered dominance of private pension schemes which offer nothing to most people and a form of unequal competition between those same funds and a state earnings-related scheme which attempts to mimic them. We must of course oppose the privatization plans of the Conservatives and the intensification of inequality in old age which lies behind those plans. The principle of state pensions provision should be defended, but an emphasis on developing such provision primarily through earnings-related payments is incompatible with an egalitarian politics. It may be difficult for the left to disengage from its commitment to state earnings-related pensions, but until it does so there will be no voice arguing for the principle of equality in old age.

Notes

1. V.C. Fry, E.M. Hammond and J.A. Kay, *Taxing Pensions*, London 1985.
2. Figures from Central Statistical Office, *Social Trends 14*, London 1984, and from Mike Reddin, *Can We Afford Our Future?*, Mitcham 1985.
3. National Consumer Council, *Of Benefit to All*, London 1984.
4. HMSO, *Social Security Statistics 1984*, London 1985.
5. These are 1982 figures, from *Social Security Statistics 1984*.
6. Reddin, *Can We Afford Our Future?*
7. Parliamentary Question, *Hansard*, 8 February 1985.
8. Fry, Hammond and Kay.
9. Parliamentary Question, *Hansard*, 7 February 1985.
10. Quoted in Social Security Advisory Committee, *First Annual Report*, London 1983.
11. *Social Security No. 2 Act* 1980.
12. HMSO, *Government Actuary's Quinquennial Review of the National Insurance Fund* (HC 451), London 1982.
13. R.M. Altmann and A.B. Atkinson, *State Pensions, Taxation and Retirement Income 1981-2031* in M. Fogarty ed. *Retirement Policy: the next fifty years*, London 1982.
14. 'Source of Calculations', *Hansard*, 5 July 1983.
15. All figures from E. Johnston, *Pension Schemes*, Survey of the Government Actuary, London 1979.

16. Contribution figures assume employee is earning more than £130 a week.

17. See Mike Reddin, 'Taxation and Pensions', in C. Sandford, C. Pond and R. Walker eds., *Taxation and Social Policy*.

18. Reddin, *Can We Afford Our Future?*

19. Johnstone, *Pension Schemes*.

20. Richard Minns, *Pension Funds and British Capitalism*, London 1980.

21. *Guardian*, 25 January 1983.

22. *Banking on the City*, CIS Report No. 33, London 1983.

23. *Guardian*, 14 April 1984.

24. Richard Minns, *Taking Over the City*, London 1982.

25. Nicholas Barr, *Myths My Grandpa Taught Me*.

26. *The Times*, 6 April 1983.

6

Sickness and Disability

The Present System

In London during the early part of 1985, the Spastics Society produced a series of posters highlighting the needs of some disabled people and the difficulties they face in active participation. One poster which effectively made this point unfortunately also focused on an inaccurate but popular image of disability. It concerned public access and depicted a young white man in a wheelchair at the steps of a public toilet, with the slogan, 'As far as I'm concerned it's neither public nor convenient.' The idea that the typical disabled person is a young white man in a wheelchair is a common misconception. There are more than twice as many disabled women as men; nearly two-thirds of all severely disabled people are aged sixty-five or over; and the biggest single cause of disability is arthritis. Ignorance of the numbers of disabled people, their needs and problems is reflected in the general lack of provision for them.

There are five groups whose needs are most neglected: carers of disabled people; children; the elderly; people who are mentally handicapped; and people who are mentally ill. Those with mental handicap or mental illnesses tend to be ignored by the social security system, which concentrates more on physical disabilities. More generally, mental handicap and mental illness are often lumped together, as they are under mental health legislation. Yet the needs of a mentally handicapped person with an IQ below the normal range are quite different from those of a mentally ill person, for example, someone suffering from anxiety or depression. Children are another group whose special needs are often ignored. It is wrongly assumed that, as all children need care and attention, the special needs of disabled children can be discounted. Those who care for disabled people, usually women, have their exploitation sanctioned by the assumption that it is their natural duty to provide care for dependent relatives. Elderly people with disabilities make up the largest group of disabled people: their disabilities and needs are ignored by attributing them to 'old age'.

We have already discussed the position of carers in general in Chapter 4. In this chapter we look more specifically at the provision of care for disabled people. We also attempt to develop an approach to income maintenance which is sensitive to the needs of all disabled people. We reject the arbitrary exclusion of some groups from entitlement to many benefits which characterizes the present social security system. The main focus of the chapter is disability, but we also discuss sickness, particularly as it overlaps with disability in the income maintenance system.

Extent of Disability

Work is currently underway by the Office of Population Censuses and Surveys (OPCS) to carry out a new national survey of disabilities. The survey itself was started at the beginning of March 1985, but its findings will not be available for a long time after the survey is completed. The most recent official estimates are from an OPCS survey carried out during 1968/9. There were then over 3 million people lacking part or all of a limb or having a defective limb, organ or mechanism. This total included over 1.1 million who had substantial difficulty in carrying out the normal functions of daily living.[1] This was undoubtedly an underestimate of the numbers of disabled people. The survey did not cover blind, deaf or mentally handicapped people; it also excluded children under sixteen and people in institutions. Other research suggests that there are nearly 10 million people of all ages with disabilities, including over half a million children. Three million disabled people have a very severe, severe or appreciable disablement.[2] The OPCS survey found that 65 per cent of those with disabilities were aged sixty-five or over, two-thirds of whom were women. As nearly half of all women sixty-five and over live by themselves, this large group have an acute need for caring services or help with the cost of care.[3]

Disability is strongly linked to poverty. The OPCS survey showed that 30 per cent of people with disabilities were living on supplementary benefit (SB). In Greenwich 30 per cent of all households including at least one seriously disabled person are poor: this measure of deprivation applied a common standard to all families and so took no account of the special needs and extra expenses incurred by disabled people.[4] Both the OPCS survey and the research done by Peter Townsend showed that, regardless of age, poverty was strongly related to the level of disability.[5]

Who Gets What?

Most of the benefits already described in this book can be claimed by sick and disabled people. Below we summarize the benefits of special relevance to them.

(1) *Sickness.* Statutory Sick Pay (SSP) is the benefit paid to most employees during the first eight weeks of any sickness. SSP is effectively a state benefit: although administered by employers, the full costs are met by the DHSS. Payments are set on an earnings-related basis at three levels: £28.25, £35.45 and £42.25. These levels are not increased in respect of children and partners. Those who have exhausted their entitlement to SSP (or those who were not entitled at all) can claim sickness benefit at a rate of £27.25 for a single person. Unlike SSP, sickness benefit is contributory and administered by the DHSS.

(2) *Long-term Sickness Disability.* After twenty-eight weeks of sickness, invalidity benefit (IVB) becomes payable to those who have satisfied the contribution conditions for sickness benefit. IVB consists of a pension, an allowance related to the claimant's age at the time the incapacity for work started and an earnings-related component. IVB lasts for as long as the incapacity for work lasts and usually entails a medical assessment by a DHSS doctor. So, for example, a single person who falls sick before s/he reaches the age of forty and satisfies the conditions for IVB would receive a pension of £34.25, an allowance of £7.50 and maybe a small earnings-related component. Those not able to work for a prolonged period due to sickness or disability and not satisfying the contribution conditions for IVB may be able to claim severe disablement allowance (SDA). To satisfy its conditions a claimant must have been incapable of work continuously since before their twentieth birthday. Alternatively they must show they are 80 per cent disabled (according to the disablement test used in the industrial injuries scheme). Only those with very serious disabilities pass this test, yet the rate of benefit is only £21.50 for a single person.

(3) *Industrial Injury.* Any employee injured at work or contracting one of the listed industrial diseases is covered by the Industrial Injuries Scheme. In general the special benefits in the scheme can be claimed on top of the normal benefits for sick and disabled people. In addition to SSP, those covered can claim sickness and invalidity benefits without having to meet the contribution conditions. A disablement pension is paid after twenty-eight weeks. This pension is tax-free and assessed according to the percentage level of disablement resulting from the injury or sickness. The top rate of 100 per cent disablement for anyone over eighteen is £58.40. This reduces proportionately in 10 per cent bands and any assessment below 20 per cent is paid as a one-off lump sum. Those assessed as less than 100 per cent disabled are compensated for their loss of earning power by a special hardship allowance, up to a maximum of £22.24 a week. There are other allowances available for special needs under this scheme. More preferential treatment is given to those injured at war through the war pensions scheme.

(4) *Care.* A disabled person who has needed substantial care for at least six months can claim attendance allowance. It is non-contributory and payable at two rates: £19.60 for someone who needs frequent care with their bodily functions or constant supervision during either the day or night; and £28.60 for someone who needs this care twenty-four hours a day. It is not payable in respect of children under two. People who are giving substantial care of at least thirty-five hours a week to a disabled person in receipt of attendance allowance can claim invalid care allowance (ICA) at a rate of £21.50 a week (equivalent to an hourly rate of 61p). This benefit is not payable to married women or women in couples — although this rule is being challenged in the European Courts.

(5) *Mobility.* Mobility allowance is paid to disabled people who are unable or virtually unable to walk as a result of a physical disability. Those aged under five or over sixty-six cannot claim mobility allowance, but those people already receiving it at the age of sixty-five can continue to get it for the following ten years.

(6) *Means-tested Benefits.* The levels of most of the benefits described above leave the people claiming them in need of means-tested benefits as well. After a year of not being able to work, sick and disabled people become eligible for the higher long-term rate of supplementary benefit (SB). The rate can be increased by small weekly additions for special needs such as extra heating and special diets. Both sickness benefit and invalidity pension are paid below the appropriate level of SB. Carers may also be able to claim SB without the usual requirement to be available for work. Housing benefit (HB) can be increased by a small addition for people who are, or could be, registered disabled.

(7) *Residence Conditions.* Severe disablement allowance has an extremely restrictive residence condition: the claimant must have been resident in Great Britain for ten years out of the last twenty. Other benefits, in particular non-contributory ones, also have residence conditions but not nearly as stringent.

The different groups described above are all divided by their relationship to the labour market and a clear hierarchy emerges which has no bearing on the extent of the disability of the claimant. In order to illustrate this point, consider the example of a single woman aged forty who has had an injury and consequently has a back problem, serious enough for her to be treated as incapable of working. The benefits she gets depend on the precise circumstances in which she first became disabled. If the injury was the result of an accident at work, she can claim benefits under the industrial injuries scheme as well as sickness and invalidity benefits. However, if the injury didn't take place at work, even though she was employed at the time, she can only claim sickness and invalidity benefits. She is not covered by the industrial injuries scheme, and is even worse off if the injury took place at a time when she had not recently made NI contributions. In this case, she can only claim severe disablement allowance. In all these situations, no matter what the circumstance of the injury, she can claim attendance and mobility allowance if her disability meets their stringent conditions, and means-tested benefits on low-income grounds. She is far more likely to have to resort to means-tested benefits if the injury is not an industrial one and more likely still if she cannot claim contributory benefits.

Another example illustrates how the needs of disabled children, particularly those with a mental handicap, are ignored. Parents of a mentally handicapped baby receive no special benefit for the first two years. They are then able to claim attendance allowance under very restrictive conditions. At the age of five, the child becomes eligible for mobility allowance, but the parents will have to show at least that the mental handicap has a physical cause and that, as a result, the child cannot walk at all.

All surveys show a very low level of take-up of benefits among disabled people.[6] This is partly due to ignorance of the benefits and the reluctance of many claimants to go on to the means test. But disabled people are in a particularly difficult position in discovering and enforcing their rights. Access to DHSS offices is very bad and surviving the queues is a trial of strength for anyone. Regular home visits to investigate the needs of long-term claimants such as disabled people and pensioners have been cut back.

The system strongly reflects the pro-capitalist principles of income maintenance described at the beginning of Chapter 2. To begin with, the principle of compensation determines that those injured through war or work receive higher and better benefits than others with the same level of disability. War pensions even give preferential treatment according to rank. The result is to divide off the better organized and more powerful groups from other disabled people. Secondly, the insurance principle determines that those who have an adequate contribution record are eligible for higher benefits. This principle discriminates against those who have never worked (including many congenitally disabled people) and recent immigrants. Thirdly, the Tory strategy of privatization has given an even more important role to occupational welfare. The introduction and proposed extension to twenty-eight weeks of SSP illustrates this strategy. Payments for sickness — once clearly a state responsibility — are now administered by employers. Although employees have in theory a legal entitlement, in practice many elements of SSP are subject to the goodwill of employers. An individual employee can complain to the DHSS about nonpayment or illegal administration, but the DHSS has no direct powers of enforcement over employers. An employee's only recourse would be to use the cumbersome county court procedure. The Commons Public Accounts Committee recently reported that one in three payments under SSP were wrong and that employers with occupational sick pay schemes had benefited disproportionately from its introduction.[7]

Fourthly, means-tested benefits are a major source of income for sick and disabled people. We have referred above to the large number of disabled people
who rely on HB and SB. We argued in Chapter 2 that there is an analogy
between means-testing and charity, and that in general the role of charity has
been supplanted by state welfare. However, in the case of disability, charity
itself still retains a more important role than in any other area. The unchallenged
assumption is that disabled people can rely on private charity for services and
even financial support. The Family Fund was set up in 1973 following the tha-
lidomide scandal to give benefits to severely disabled children. It is administered
by the Rowntree Memorial Trust, but funded by the government. The mota-
bility scheme is another example: the government can pay mobility allowance
to a private charity which in return leases a car to the claimant. The running
costs have to be met out of the claimant's other income, and the government,
by using a charity, evades responsibility for the mobility of disabled people.

Finally, the state relies extensively on voluntary support from family and
relatives to make up the shortfall in services and benefits for disabled people.
The lack of benefits for carers frequently causes poverty to spread to a much
wider group. The assumption that the family should provide care is explicit in
the rules for invalid care allowance, which excludes married women. It is implicit in the levels of benefit. It is clearly impossible for someone who receives the
higher rate of attendance allowance to pay for twenty-four-hour care that they
need out of an allowance of £28.60 a week. It represents an hourly rate of 17p.

Both attendance and mobility allowance appear to depart from the principles
described above in so far as they relate more directly to the needs of the claimants. Yet they both operate an oppressive degree of selectivity through the
methods of assessment of need. In particular a pass/fail test of disability is
applied to these benefits. Effectively a claimant is treated as either entirely disabled or not disabled at all. One recent decision refused a woman mobility
allowance because, although she could not walk unaided from one place to
another, she could still go through the motions of moving her legs in the manner required for walking. The fact that she could not make use of this ability
was ruled to be irrelevant to the test.[8] Rejection in circumstances like this is
incomprehensible to a disabled person, who experiences it as a denial of her/his
disability. S/he still has to continue to rely on friends and family for voluntary
support. This pass/fail test has another effect which places claimants in an
impossible no-win situation. In order to qualify s/he will have to demonstrate
how incapable s/he is, yet to survive on a day-to-day basis the opposite
approach is essential. Survival becomes treated as evidence of self-sufficiency
and the only way of getting a much needed benefit is to play the game of help-
lessness, with all the humiliation that involves. The process is made worse by
the power exercised by doctors who are often unsympathetic to the needs and
aspirations of disabled people and who have at best a sketchy knowledge of the

benefit system. The restrictive conditions and assessments of these benefits prevent many people in need from getting them. In May 1984 there were only 319,650 people getting mobility allowance and slightly more getting attendance allowance.

Employment and Incapacity

We have argued above that the system of benefits for sick and disabled people closely follows positive pro-capitalist principles. There is a negative pro-capitalist principle that the income maintenance system should disturb as little as possible the operation of the labour market. In Chapter 3 we explored the way in which the labour market depends on a compulsion to work which is enforced through low benefits paid to unemployed people. The test of incapacity for work applied to benefits for sickness fits into the same overall framework. Treatment of the long-term sick diverges dramatically from that of the long-term unemployed, but only on the basis of the complete separation of the chronically sick from the labour market. This creates two problems for the chronically sick: firstly, a rigorous incapacity test; and, secondly, what can be called an 'incapacity trap'.

Although there is legally only one test of incapacity which should apply throughout the whole period of sickness, the DHSS in fact applies a much stricter test to those who have gone on to, or are about to go on to, the higher long-term benefits (IVB after six months or long-term rate SB after a year). The DHSS initally accepts sick notes issued by a GP, but after twenty-eight weeks of sickness these are often treated as unreliable. Claimants are called for medical examination by a DHSS regional medical officer (RMO). The RMO checks whether there is any kind of work which the claimant could conceivably carry out and, if so, decides that they are capable of work. Unless this is successfully challenged, the claimant is pronounced unemployed rather than sick and their benefit is cut.

The rigour of the test combined with the rigid distinction between those who are capable of any work and those who are not produces the 'incapacity trap'. The long-term sick are forced to choose between having no work and preserving their benefits which are superior (by comparison), or re-entering the labour market. If, for example, they take an undemanding part-time job, even for just a few hours a week, the DHSS are likely to treat them as no longer sick and consequently discontinue their IVB.[9] Having experimented unsuccessfully with work, a chronically sick person has an even harder task convincing the DHSS that s/he is eligible for sickness benefits.

Someone deemed capable of work by the RMO can register as disabled and theoretically qualify for help from the disablement resettlement officer in finding a job. Employers with twenty or more workers are supposed to employ a 3 per cent quota of disabled people. The quota system has been in operation for over forty years but it is largely ignored by employers and enforcement is feeble. Up to 1980 there had only been ten prosecutions for failure to employ disabled people and in the seven cases where fines were imposed the total sum was only £334.[10] Given this official lack of support, many disabled people looking for work do not bother to register. The register is divided into two sections — one for those capable of working in ordinary employment and the other for those able to work only in sheltered workshops. Sheltered workshops frequently provide menial repetitive work, such as stuffing envelopes, at exploitative rates of pay. For example, in May 1982 Brent Council was paying sixty mentally and physically handicapped people 80p a day to fold and fill envelopes for Grunwick's, and had been doing so for the past eight years.[11] This period included the Grunwick dispute in 1977 — a strike which the council supported. The excuse given by Brent Council for paying such low wages was that it is the maximum allowed before SB is reduced. The benefits system requires that sick and disabled people who want to do some form of work either accept pitiful wages or unemployment.

A Benefit of a Kind

One defence of the inadequacy of benefits for disabled people is that these are complemented by local services. The Chronically Sick and Disabled Persons Act 1970 obliges local authorities to compile a register of chronically sick and disabled people within their area and to assess their needs. Many disabled people don't know about the register and others do not apply to be on it because the services provided are often minimal. The better authorities provide services such as aids in the home (for example, a telephone), adaption to houses for access and mobility, holidays, home helps, day centres and adult training centres. The Act leaves each local authority to define need in its own way and so the level and range of services diffr enormously. For example, in 1977/8 one local authority was adapting 8.3 private houses per thousand, another was adapting none at all: each was treated as complying with the Act.[12] Local authorities are now being expected to provide 'community care' schemes in response to the closing down of hospitals and long-stay institutions, but with insufficient extra resources. The House of Commons Social Services Select Committee commented on the plan to move 100,000 mentally handicapped and ill people from hospitals into the community: 'Any fool can close a long-stay hospital, it takes more time and trouble to do it properly and compassionately. The Minister must ensure that mental illness or mental handicap hospital provision is not reduced without demonstrably adequate alternative services being provided beforehand.'[13] There is no sign of the government responding to this call.

Services are scarce, undemocratic and operated by professionalized social service departments according to the requirements of administrative efficiency. Disabled people are not given an opportunity to impose their needs and wishes on the services. There are two broad strategies for overcoming these problems: one to democratize and extend service; the other to provide cash benefits to enable disabled people to purchase the services they want. We discuss these strategies in the second part of this chapter.

New Ideas for a Better System

In the same way as for other people, the basic weekly income for sick and disabled people not in work would be provided by a positional benefit. Like all positional benefits, this 'incapacity benefit' would be assessed individually without means or contribution tests. It would be paid at the same flat-rate as all other positional benefits, including unemployment benefit. This would remove the 'incapacity trap', because there would be no financial discrimination between those incapable of work and the unemployed. Indeed it would be possible and desirable to accommodate partial incapacity within this framework. So, someone capable of doing some work on a part-time basis could receive incapacity benefit for that part of the week not spent at work and like everyone else they would earn at least the minimum hourly wage while at work. Someone entitled to partial incapacity benefit who could not find suitable part-time work could claim a combination of unemployment and incapacity benefits. As we stated in Chapter 4, we also propose a positional carers' benefit for those caring for disabled people. Similarly, this could be paid on a partial basis if the care required was not full-time.

In Chapter 2 we discussed that, although needs generally have to be assessed on an average basis, the benefit system must take account of particular needs which give rise to extra costs. Otherwise the effect on some groups which have above-average living costs would be to depress their living standards below the generally accepted average. This problem affects anyone with above-average needs on a minimum income: not only those on benefit but also those on a minimum wage. We now turn to look at the ways in which the needs of sick and disabled people generally exceed the average and ways in which these needs could fairly be assessed for income maintenance purposes. This assessment of need could form the basis of a cost-related benefit — a 'disability costs allowance' — which could go towards meeting the extra expenses which disabled people incur.

The 1975 United Nations Declaration of the Rights of Disabled Persons emphasized that disabled people have: a right to economic and social security and to a decent standard of living; the right to employment; the right to live with members of their families; and the right to participate in all social, creative or recreational activities.[14] The spirit of this declaration should be the basis for assessing the needs of disabled people for income maintenance. However, there are degrees of disability which cannot be compensated for financially. The aim should be to set a level of benefit in order to try to maximize participation as far as practicable. The present system already recognizes certain needs and activities which are seen as important and involve extra expense, such as the need for care (attendance allowance) and the need to get about (mobility allowance). As they stand, these benefits are not only themselves inadequate but leave a whole range of other needs uncatered for. It is possible to suggest certain broad categories of need which should be covered and taken into account in determining a maximum level of disability cost allowance. An assessment of individual needs would not be required in each case — such assessments would entail an unacceptable level of selectivity. The disability cost allowance would have to relate costs on an average basis to the extent of disability.

The broad categories of need are: heating; household goods and maintenance, such as small aids and adaptations to the home, cleaning and repairs; leisure, for example, holidays or sport; mobility; care, in other words care provided by other people; personal costs, including items like the extra cost of food, clothes and the cost of shopping for goods or having them delivered; extra costs incurred by disabled parents, for example, the need to make special arrangements to take their child to school; independent care, that is, things to help disabled people look after themselves, such as a telephone.

These categories of need would have to be regularly reviewed so that they reflected new developments and changing standards of living. Disabled people would have to be closely involved in this process. Any such list is based on assumptions about what other sources of support are available. For example, we haven't included medical treatment, because it ought to be freely provided through the National Health Service (including free prescriptions). One service which could cover a number of these categories is the provision of facilitators, who could enable disabled people to participate. The position of a carer could be expanded to take on a more enabling role.

Care is an area which needs particularly careful consideration, because disabled people should have as much choice as possible in deciding how to meet their need for care. Our approach incorporates three main elements. First of all, the provision of services — such as home helps, day centres, residential homes and domiciliary nursing — should be developed. As appropriate, statutory duties should be placed on local authorities and health authorities to provide these services. This development of public services must take place with the full participation of disabled people. Otherwise the bureaucratic and alienating provision characteristic of current local authority social services would simply be reproduced and extended. But the development of such democratically controlled services would inevitably take a long period of time to complete.

Secondly, disabled people should have the option of having a carer's benefit paid to a friend or relative willing to fulfil that role — but equally they should be able to veto such an arrangement. Care given by a friend or relative should never be assumed to be sufficient without the support of caring services. Many disabled people require a level of care which it is totally unreasonable to expect one other person to provide.

Thirdly, there is a need for a benefit which would give some assistance to disabled people with the costs of privately arranged care. Consider the example of a disabled person in need of constant care, who is being cared for by a relative. This extra benefit could be used to pay someone to come in regularly and give the carer a break. Such a benefit could also be payable to those disabled people who do not wish to use — or cannot find — public services or care from a relative or friend. There is a danger that where this payment is used to substitute for other sources of full-time care it could tend to undermine caring services by enabling the better-off disabled people to buy private services. On balance, however, it is desirable, since it would give disabled people a greater choice when faced with inadequate public services.

An Enabling Assessment

The question clearly arises how the degree of an individual's disability should be related to the general categories of need in order to allow an appropriate assessment of the amount of disability cost allowance required? The World Health Organization has suggested three methods of measuring disability, taking the form of a progression: firstly, impairment, which can most easily be described as parts of the body that don't work; secondly, disablement, the inability to carry out certain activities; and, thirdly, handicap, the inability to perform certain roles. All these tests have been used in the social security system and it is possible to see how they work in practice. The industrial injuries scheme uses an impairment test ('loss of faculty'). It is easily and precisely measurable in those cases to which it applies: the present scheme has a chart which states that, for example, the amputation of an arm from 20.5 centimetres from the tip of the acromion to less than 11.5 centimetres below the tip of the olecranon constitutes a 70 per cent impairment. However, for the majority of people such a precise measurement is impossible. How could the disability of someone with crippling arthritis be measured on a test of impairment? Impairment tests are notoriously inadequate in measuring nervous disorders, particularly if the severity varies from day to day as in the case of multiple sclerosis. A test of impairment will also tend to ignore the wider physical and personal consequences of disability, like pain and stress. It is, in essence, a medical test, concentrating on the immediate physical effects of a disability.

Handicap as a measurement is too general and imprecise. It involves selecting a number of activities which make up a 'role' and then measures the person's inability to perform those activities. The drawback of this test is that it involves categorizing people into culturally defined roles. The recently abolished house-wives non-contributory invalidity pension (HNCIP) categorized all married or cohabiting women as housewives. To claim HNCIP successfully, a woman had to show that she was incapable of doing housework. Yet men could claim an equivalent benefit irrespective of their ability to do housework. Clearly, if a married woman's ability to cook and clean is treated as important, the same test should apply to a business executive. The generality of the test of housework was also used as a method of excluding women from benefit.

A test of disablement avoids some of the pitfalls of a handicap test by focusing on separate activities which a disabled person cannot perform, rather than on culturally defined roles. It is also highly flexible in that it enables the extent of disability to be assessed with regard to the most appropriate selection of distinct disablements — for example, inability to walk, shop, bath oneself and so on. Mobility allowance provides an example of such a test: can the claimant walk or not? But it also highlights the fact that tests of disablement can be applied in a highly restrictive manner. One of the main drawbacks of the mobility allowance test of disability is that it is a pass/fail test. Yet in reality disability is not experienced totally or not at all — it is a matter of degree. Any assessment of disability has to recognize this.

We propose a test whereby the degree of each disablement would be assessed on a points scale. This points scale would allow disablements to be weighted to give rise to a particular measure of disability. The weighting given to each disablement would depend on a judgement of its 'importance'. For income maintenance purposes the 'importance' of a disablement is the extent to which it gives rise to needs which in turn cause additional expenditure. Thus the index of disablements would have to be related to a categorization of needs such as the one we proposed earlier. To take a simple example, the weight to be given to a disablement such as difficulty in walking would take account of needs for general mobility, heating (because the disabled person would spend more time at home), leisure (because these activities involve being able to get around), etc. Using this method, it would be unnecessary to have separate benefits for different needs. Someone with a mental handicap, needing only a little help with mobility costs, but more help with personal care, might receive the same level of benefit as a pensioner with arthritis whose main need was in the area of mobility. It might be sensible automatically to pay the very elderly a certain level of disability cost allowance on the assumption that they would experience some degree of disability.

The best way of ensuring the dignity of disabled people claiming this benefit is to have some form of self-assessment, similar to the principle of income tax returns. Ensuring a common standard would require that it should be complemented by other assessments; these could be provided by the claimant's GP or a carer. The burden of proof would be shifted away from the claimant to the benefit authority, as is already the case with war pensions. It would be up to the benefit authority to show that the claimant could carry out a particular activity rather than the claimant having to justify her/his disability.

Apart from the obstacles which the social security system places in the way of disabled people trying to work, jobs are not usually available. It would be necessary to strengthen the quota system by the introduction of fines and to provide grants and subsidies to adapt workplaces for disabled workers. The aim should be to integrate disabled people into the work-force so that there would no longer be any need for segregated sheltered workshops. Instead of stuffing envelopes, disabled workers could be using the latest technology to enable them to do the same range of jobs as other workers.

In this chapter we have developed proposals based on the assumption that a form of selectivity is inevitable in income maintenance to meet the particular needs of disabled people. The benefits we have proposed would not be means-tested or contributory, and they would be separately assessed without age or residence restrictions. But they would entail a selective assessment of the degree of disability experienced by particular individuals. If such selective assessment is unavoidable, it is also essential to consider how it could be carried out in a way that preserves the dignity and independence of disabled people, and how the benefits paid could meet their needs in a way that the current system so blatantly fails to do. The test of disability we propose, linked to payment of disability cost allowance, would provide flexibility to meet the needs of groups such as the young and old, people with mental handicaps and those with mental illnesses — groups whose needs are largely ignored at present. Incorporating the payment of adequate incapacity and carers' benefits, the system we propose would very substantially improve the position of disabled people: but to meet their needs most effectively it would have to be introduced not only for disabled people, but under their direct control.

Notes

1. Amelia Harris, *Handicapped and Impaired in Great Britain*, Office of Population and Census Studies Survey, London 1971.

2. Peter Townsend, *Poverty in the United Kingdom*, Harmondsworth 1979.

3. HMSO *Social Trends 14*, London 1984 Table A2.

4. Greenwich Welfare Rights Unit, *Breadline Greenwich: Welfare Rights Implications*, London 1984.

102

5. *Social Trends 14*.
6. See, for example, Birmingham Tribunal Unit, *A Fairer Deal for Fairways*, Birmingham 1984.
7. *Guardian* 30 March 1985.
8. HMSO, *Social Security Commissioner's Decision*, R(M)1/84.
9. There is provision for 'therapeutic earnings'. These are limited to a maximum of £23.50 and must be undertaken either under medical supervision or for some other good reason.
10. Alan Walker and Peter Townsend, eds., *Poverty and Disability*, Oxford 1981.
11. Derek Bishton, *The Sweatshop Report*, Nottingham 1984.
12. *The Sweatshop Report*.
13. *Guardian* 1 March 1985.
14. *The Sweatshop Report*.

'I feel more comfortable living here,' commented Mr Sumsud. At the time he was sleeping on the floor of a Camden Town Hall committee room, along with members of about eighty other families. Two weeks earlier their 'temporary' lodgings in a bed and breakfast hotel had burnt down, killing Mrs Abdul Karim and her two young children. The eighty families, mostly Asian, had been living in the hostel for several months, at a weekly cost to the council and DHSS of up to £200 per family. They were officially homeless and in priority need. Due to government-imposed cuts on housing expenditure Camden Council did not have the flats to rehouse them. While the homeless families were camping in the town hall, a Camden estate agent was informing owner-occupiers that one prudent couple had gained £10,000 by selling their home with that agent's advice. They made a tax-free capital gain on top of the money they had saved in reduced tax on their mortgage, both subsidized by the government.

These events were dramatic reminders that the combination of government policy on housing investment, the operation of the housing market itself (primarily influenced by subsidies to owner-occupiers) and the social security system together ensure that housing need fails to be met. Tens of thousands of people are chronically homeless, hundreds of thousands more live in defective homes, while others become rich on their personal investment in housing.

There is a chronic shortage of housing. Prices are being driven up constantly and the government has been able to increase rents faster than the rate of inflation. Hence more and more people, now about one in four of all households, have to claim HB for their rental costs. In contrast, owner-occupiers (and estate agents, surveyors, solicitors, etc.) make money from the housing shortage because of the resulting increase in the value of their home. The large, arbitrary and inequitable variations in the costs of housing pose critical problems for an income maintenance system: how can fair assistance with housing costs be given without resort to means tests; secondly, can it be made compatible with the efficient production and distribution of housing; and thirdly, can it take account of the different housing tenures?

The current hotch-potch of housing finance and income maintenance policies fails all these tests. They fail to stimulate the production of housing — either the building of new houses or the improvement and maintenance of the 4½ million substandard ones.[1] They help to concentrate wealth in the hands of those who are already wealthy. They fail to get adequate assistance with the cost of housing to those who are in need of it. They support a very unequal distribution of housing which bears little relation to need. Manual workers on low incomes generally live in public sector housing, with all its problems of bad conditions and management. The poorest people are usually in the worst housing of all: the hard-to-let estates and tower blocks. Black people live in the worst housing in all tenures.[2] For example, over one-third of Asian households have more than one person living in each room, compared to only 3 per cent of white households, and three-quarters of Asian households live in accommodation built before 1945, compared to only half of white households. This chapter describes these inequalities and how the income maintenance system reproduces and reinforces them.

The Present System

The following is a summary of current arrangements for assistance with housing costs:

(1) *Housing benefit (HB)*. This is a means-tested benefit for people who pay rent or general rates. It is administered by local housing authorities, but most of the bill is met by the DHSS. People on supplementary benefit (SB) receive an amount equal to their rent and rates. Others get only a proportion of their rent and rates, which rapidly decreases as their income increases.

(2) *Supplementary Benefit (SB)*. This may be granted to owner-occupiers to pay their mortgage interest (but not the capital) and they are allowed a fixed sum of £1.80 per week for maintenance and insurance costs. People over twenty-one who live in someone else's household get a fixed housing addition of £3.30 per week.

(3) *Mortgage Interest Tax Relief*. This is paid to owner-occupiers. This scheme now falls into two parts. The first is a general mortgage interest subsidy, mortgage interest relief at source (MIRAS), through which the government subsidizes a reduced rate of interest for people who buy their home, up to a maximum loan of £30,000 (this is no longer truly a tax relief as it is available to non-taxpayers). Higher-rate taxpayers can choose to pay no tax on their interest payments instead. This is worth more to them than the standard reduction in interest rates.

(4) *Capital Taxes.* Owner-occupiers are exempt from capital taxes when their house is either sold, given away or inherited.

(5) *Rent Controls.* Charging people a lower rent has a similar effect to raising their income to enable them to pay a higher rent: they have the same amount of money left to spend on other things. In the public sector, local authorities can choose, or are sometimes directed, to set a rent at a level considered to be 'fair'. Expenditure on housing revenue in excess of rental income can then be met from another source, for example, taxes or rates. In the private sector the rents charged by landlords are controlled, inadequately, by legislation which establishes fair rents for some tenancies.

(6) *'Right to Buy'.* The legislation introduced in 1980 reduced the cost of purchase, by as much as 60 per cent in some cases, of local authority houses sold to existing tenants.

(7) *Board and Lodging.* Homeless people in temporary accommodation have their costs met by sb. In April 1985 the government introduced punitive restrictions on the amount payable (often well below the actual cost) and reduced the period for which the cost of lodgings is paid to between two and eight weeks for most claimants under twenty-six.

Public Sector Housing: Rents, Rebates and 'Subsidies'

In a White Paper issued in 1965 the Labour Party argued that 'Help for those who most need it can be given only if the subsidies are in large part used to provide rebates for tenants whose means are small.'[3] They followed this in June 1967 with a circular encouraging rebate schemes. In 1972 the Conservative Housing Finance Act imposed such a means-tested scheme on all housing authorities. Both Conservative and Labour governments have recognized that putting up council rents is a straightforward way of saving central government money. Starting from the observation that some tenants with higher incomes *could* pay more rent, it was an easy step to the conclusion that they *should* pay more for their home. 'Subsidy' has been reduced and concentrated on those with the lowest incomes. Firstly, through means-tested rebate schemes, and then the housing benefit scheme introduced in 1982/3. This policy has encouraged higher-paid workers, faced with high council rents, to become owner-occupiers. This policy has been taken a stage further with the generous discounts given to those buying their council home. This process of concentrating subsidies has also led to a confusion between public investment in housing and 'subsidy' to council tenants.

The present Tory government has intensified this strategy. Council rents have increased from an average of £5.90 per week in 1979/80 to £14.77 in 1984/5 (excluding rates), an increase in real terms of about 40 per cent. Housing Associations have also been forced to increase their rents above the rate of inflation since 1972. At the same time, the total central government contribution to housing revenue expenditure fell by a staggering 85 per cent in real terms between 1979 and 1985. In 1984, for the first time, total rent rebate payments exceeded all public expenditure on local authority housing.[4] The limit on the money borrowed by English housing authorities for house building was cut from just under £5 thousand million to £1.5 thousand million (in real terms) over this same period.[5] Comparing the total national spending on council housing and the total income from rents, council housing now pays for itself and almost no new council housing is being built.

The introduction of the HB scheme in 1982/3 allowed the government to highlight and exaggerate the increase in expenditure on rebates by bringing together the two previous schemes of assistance with housing costs (SB and rent rebates).[6] The government has managed to get away with arguing that the major reason for this increase in expenditure has been the generosity of the scheme. In fact the major reasons have been increasing unemployment, lower wages and local authority rent rises — which the government itself has engineered. From here it has been an easy step for the government to argue that HB should be cut. The strategy of singling out HB for extra cuts has been ruthlessly pursued by the government. The first cuts affecting about 2¼ million of the 4½ million people on HB were introduced with the full implementation of the HB scheme in April 1983. In November that year the government announced further cuts in HB expenditure totalling £230 million per year which took effect in April 1984 (after protests, this cut was reduced to £215 million). There were yet more cuts to HB introduced in April 1985 and it seems likely that the major source of cuts resulting from the government reviews of social security will once again be the HB scheme.

One element of the 1984 cuts in HB amounts to a household means test, the type of means test so hated in the 1920s and 1930s. Relatives, working children or friends living with a tenant are now expected to contribute £6.60 per week to the rent. This amount is deducted from the claimant's HB: it represents just under half of a local authority average rent. This is usually more than the tenant himself is expected to pay after HB is taken into account.[7] Increases in the rate of withdrawal of HB have intensified the 'poverty trap'. As a result of these cuts, rebates are now restricted to those with earnings well below average or with exceptionally high rents.

Owner Occupation

People who own or who are buying the house they live in (currently over 55 per cent of all households) receive the largest amount of assistance with their housing costs, both in total and for each household. They receive tax relief on mortgate interest and exemption from capital gains tax.[8] Tax concessions to owner-occupiers are of greatest benefit to the better off and have made the private housing market the most significant area of growth in personal wealth, more than doubling over the period 1960-75. In addition to being inegalitarian, these subsidies do not promote an adequate supply of housing to meet need.

The current method of administering mortgage interest tax relief has slightly changed its effects — to the detriment of most borrowers and to the benefit of building societies and banks. The new scheme is called mortgage interest relief at source (MIRAS) and applies to the first £30,000 of a loan. Instead of reducing tax paid by deducting mortgage interest payments from taxable income, under MIRAS the interest rate is reduced directly by 30 per cent. The borrower pays lower interest out of taxed income as opposed to higher interest out of untaxed income. This means that people not paying tax also receive relief for their mortgage payments. The effect of this administrative change is to increase the real cost of mortgages to basic rate taxpayers, because they receive less relief at the beginning of their mortgage (when it is worth more to them). People paying tax at higher rates can choose to have tax relief in the usual way. This is worth more to them, because interest payments are offset against income which is otherwise taxable at rates of between 40 and 60 per cent. The total amount paid to owner-occupiers in 1984/5 as mortgage interest tax relief was about £3.5 thousand million.

In 1983/4 more than half of this huge amount of money went to people with incomes over £10,000 per year, a figure considerably above average earnings. The amount of relief *increases* as income increases; someone earning between £5,000 and £6,000 gained on average £175 per year in tax relief, whereas someone earning over £20,000 gained about £830 per year, nearly five times as much. This intervention in the housing market has a favoured place in the Tory strategy. The Chancellor, before the 1985 budget, was publicly warned off making an attempt to reclaim any part of the £3,500 million mortgage interest tax relief by Margaret Thatcher herself. One of the government's first acts on re-election in 1983 was to increase the maximum mortgage qualifying for tax relief from £25,000 to £30,000, a policy of benefit to only 9 per cent of borrowers, primarily those on higher incomes.

Owner-ocupiers do not only gain from the subsidy to interest payments. The value of a house increases each year, and most years its value will increase faster than inflation, so that simple possession of the house generates a real capital gain. Since the war, houses have increased in value by eighteen times (retail prices have increased eleven times).[9] Increases in the value of personal wealth — capital gains — are taxed at the rate of 30 per cent, but the gains from house sales are exempted. The total amount gained by owner-occupiers was estimated to be a further £2.5 thousand million in 1984/5.[10] It is argued that most owner-occupiers never see this capital gain; they usually have to buy a new home when they sell up. However, a survey of owner-occupiers selling homes in 1973 found that 60 per cent of those who moved from one owner-occupied house to another realized at least £500 of their sales proceeds in cash, and 16 per cent realized over £3,000. Moreover, the capital gain is always realized eventually, even if it is transferred to the owner's heirs after his/her death (for which there is a £67,000 exemption).

The 60 per cent discount to council tenants buying their existing home favours better-off tenants in regular employment who can afford a mortgage and those who happen to be tenants of the better council properties. Other tenants lose out, because the nicer homes are sold off and councils cannot afford to replace them — a total of 621,300 public sector homes were sold between 1979 and 1984.[11] The Tories seem to have gained considerably from this policy. One opinion poll suggested that 59 per cent of those who voted Labour in 1979 and who subsequently bought their council house switched to supporting the Conservative Party in 1983 — votes that had cost other tax payers a large amount in cash subsidies.[12]

Private Rented Housing

Private tenants, including people in temporary bed-and-breakfast accommodation, get the worst housing deal in every respect. Their housing costs are highest, they live in the worst and most dangerous physical conditions and they have the least security of tenure. Few people who have any choice rent privately if they can possibly avoid it. A Greater London Council survey showed that ethnic minority private tenants are additionally disadvantaged in a variety of ways: they are more likely to live in the central city area where rents are higher; they reported almost three times the level of harassment compared to white households; and more black people live in furnished accommodation which is generally less secure. Another survey showed that ethnic minority households were far more likely to be sharing basic amenities, for example, 28.2 per cent of African and 12.6 per cent of Asian households compared to only 2.8 per cent overall.[13] HB paid to private tenants in the form of rent allowances totalled only £138 million in 1983/4. Excluding those on SB there were 300,000 recipients. The relatively large amount per claimant, £460 per year, indicates the high level of private sector rents.

Board and lodging accommodation is the growth area of the private rented sector; more people are spending longer in hostels and bed-and-breakfast hotels. Government housing policy is forcing more and more people to rely on this sort of temporary accommodation; yet it refuses to accept full responsibility for the bill. As with HB, the government's response has been to respond to increased expenditure, because there are more claimants, by cutting the amount each person can claim and excluding some people altogether. To the extent that such temporary accommodation is needed, it should be provided by local authorities as part of their housing programme and funded accordingly.[14]

The proportion of privately-rented homes has declined from a high point of 90 per cent of the total housing stock at the end of the First World War to about 12 per cent.[15] The introduction of rent allowances in 1972 has not stopped the decline in the supply of privately rented housing. On the contrary, the number of households renting privately fell by over one-third from 1971 to 1981. Private sector rents are notoriously high. The GLC survey discovered that at least half of all new lettings were made outside the controls of the Rent Acts. Commenting on this, a representative of the Small Landlords Association said he was surprised that so many new lettings were *within* the Rent Acts.[16]

The government turns a blind eye to landlords charging excessive rents and then partially mitigates the worst effects of this through the rent allowances scheme. As with so many aspects of the housing finance system, the evidence suggests that increased payments on rent allowances to landlords are not ploughed back in increased investment in housing. A typical example is Paul Cowie, the one-time owner and manager of the Princes Lodge hostel in Tower Hamlets, London, a notorious profiteer from SB. He bought and restored a Gothic castle with extensive grounds in County Durham for around £750,000, a sum roughly equal to one year's income from his 200-room hostel, where claimants shared four to a room.

The Politics of Housing Expenditure

A lot of people try to overcome the difficulties of understanding housing expenditure by attempting to force a unitary analysis on the system. The temptation to find a common framework for analysis is great. It seems to allow direct comparisons to be made between the amount of money paid to each owner-occupier and to each tenant. Such an approach requires a single definition of subsidy. The one commonly used relates to the notion of 'economic rent' — the rent that would have to be charged in order to get a return on an investment in housing equal to general investment elsewhere. Economic rent is a wholly abstract concept relating to the idealized behaviour of 'rational capitalists'. It treats private renting, only 7 per cent of the market, as a standard in its measure of owner-occupiers' and council tenants' costs. Economic rent is not a useful tool for the analysis we require.

Moreover the term 'subsidy' is itself suspect: it does not distinguish between housing expenditure that produces a socially owned asset and housing expenditure which produces personal profit. For us this distinction is fundamental, for it challenges the basis of Tory propaganda that spending on public housing is a 'cost'. We argue instead that it creates an asset, that it is an investment. Moreover there is an important political issue at stake in addition to these analytical points. The comparison of one housing sector with another to decide who is getting the most subsidy leads to a 'politics of envy' approach which will always favour the right, whose politics thrive on envy, personal competition and division.

Government spending on housing can result in one or both of two outcomes. Firstly, it can affect the supply of housing, for example, the government can build houses itself, it can encourage others to do so, or it can encourage underoccupation. We consider that housing expenditure should have as one objective to provide and maintain an adequate supply of housing. Secondly, housing expenditure can affect the cost of housing to individual householders. Expenditure in this area should have the income maintenance objectives outlined in Chapter 2. To what extent does the present system of housing expenditure which we have described meet these objectives? It is possible to consider each sector in turn and review the effects of housing expenditure in that sector. Our conclusion is that the present system of housing expenditure doesn't meet socialist objectives.

The exchequer and rate fund contributions to local authority housing revenue accounts are used to make a council's annual housing budget 'balance' after rental income and costs are taken into account. As the bulk of housing revenue expenditure is on debt charges it is fair to see these contributions as directly paying for the construction, improvement and maintenance of council housing. However the Conservative government has restricted this investment expenditure to such an extent that virtually no new housing is being constructed at the moment. Only recently has this expenditure given rise to some personal profit because of discounts on council house sales.

The variety of tax reliefs enjoyed by owner-occupiers are the largest single area of housing expenditure. This expenditure simply encourages house prices to rise more quickly and encourages little new house construction. Whilst housing remains in short supply, prices are likely to rise to the maximum that prospective purchasers can afford, which is itself related to the level of tax relief. A similar analysis applies to capital gains tax relief.[17] Tax concessions do have an income maintenance effect of sorts in that some people on low income are helped to buy their own home: but they help the rich far more, distributing the money uncontrollably. They also encourage owners to 'trade up' into larger and costlier homes to continue to take advantage of the concessions. This under-occupation reduces supply.

Government expenditure on HB at first sight looks as if it reduces the cost of housing to tenants. However, it involves a punitive means test, which is becoming increasingly restrictive. Furthermore this judgement overlooks the government's power to fix public sector rents and decrease direct investment in housing: rent rebates are part of a strategy for shifting the burden for paying off past debts on housing investment from central government to tenants on all but the lowest incomes. We have argued that the rent allowance scheme has not arrested the decline of the private rented sector. So clearly housing expenditure in this sector has not increased the supply of housing. As an income maintenance scheme it has all the faults of the rest of HB.

Tory Policies

The policy of the current Tory administration has been to intensify inequalities in the housing market and corresponding inequalities in assistance with housing costs. It has done nothing to alleviate the chronic shortage of housing. Public sector housing investment has been cut and restricted, tax exemptions to owner-occupiers have been maintained (and increased in the case of mortgage interest tax relief) and HB has been restricted to the poorest tenants as rents have increased. The government is using the various mechanisms of housing expenditure to influence people's choice of housing between tenures, to ensure that, by and large, owner-occupiers will be better off than tenants. The Tory strategy aims to make council housing undesirable — to make council housing into welfare housing. Tory objectives were revealed in a letter sent on Margaret Thatcher's behalf before the 1979 election to a council tenant who complained about the quality of her council flat.

> Dear Mrs Collingwood,
> I hope you will not think me too blunt if I say that it may well be that your Council accommodation is unsatisfactory, but considering the fact that you have been unable to buy your own accommodation you are lucky to have been given something, which the rest of us are paying for out of our taxes.
>
> With good wishes,
> Matthew Parris

Money for Housing

> An increasing number of people want to own their own home. The government welcomes this trend and intend to continue to support home ownership by maintaining the current arrangements for tax relief ... For most people owning one's own home is a basic and natural desire ... The strategy [of this government] is based on increasing owner occupation, and on a developing public sector to meet the housing needs of those who cannot or do not wish to become owner occupiers.

This is not an extract from a Conservative manifesto; it comes from the Labour government's 1977 discussion paper on housing! Peter Shore was formulating a strategy for Labour which promotes owner occupation as the normal form of tenure and relegates council housing to a residual role. No wonder it has been so easy for the Tories to undermine council housing when its potential defenders are so ambivalent. The electoral obsession with home owners has diverted attention away from the crucial income maintenance considerations of housing expenditure: ensuring that everyone can afford the housing they need.

By itself income maintenance cannot achieve that objective, so a central plank of the policy must be investment to increase the supply of housing. Public expenditure on housing, like expenditure on the National Health Service or on education, is an investment to everyone's benefit. With more people becoming homeless each year and housing conditions deteriorating in all sectors, there is enormous scope for investment. Building is a very effective way of creating jobs: it is estimated that £500 million invested in housing would create at least 37,000 jobs.[18]

There are two ways of ensuring that people can afford the housing they need. One is to reduce costs, the other is to increase incomes. Increased investment would, in the long term, reduce the cost of housing in all sectors. But even with greatly increased housing investment it would take time for the increased supply to reduce costs substantially. It is essential to have some other means of helping with housing costs. We will look at each sector in turn to see how this can be achieved, starting with public housing.

One immediate and effective step would be to fix a national maximum rent. One of the chief advantages of this is that levels of benefit and the minimum wage could be linked to the maximum rent. The income maintenance positional benefit for those caring for children, the unemployed, disabled or elderly people would include a fixed amount for housing, sufficient to cover at least the average local authority rent for a single person. Similarly the minimum wage, net of tax, should be at a level sufficient to cover this same amount of rent. Where two or more people live together they could combine their individual amounts for housing costs to pay the total rent. A proportion of child benefit would also have to be attributed to rental costs for the child: this could be a smaller amount than for an adult because children never live alone. This would reduce the need for any individually assessed payments in respect of high housing costs.

One way of financing a maximum rent policy would be through a national system of 'rent-pooling' — councils which made a 'profit' on their housing because their outstanding debts were small could pass money to areas with higher debt charges to help balance their accounts. This system would also require a minimum national rent to be fixed as well. Such a system of maximum and minimum rents would make a solution to the problems of housing costs far simpler. However, there would still be variations in people's housing costs, for example, due to under-occupation. Therefore we make the pessimistic assumption that there would be such a degree of variation in cost that it would be unreasonable to expect people to meet their housing costs without further assistance.

Some form of income maintenance related specifically to the cost of housing would be required. Let's call this further assistance a housing costs allowance. It would cover a proportion of the excess costs of a person's housing above the standard amount allowed for in positional benefits and the minimum wage. It would be taxable, but not means-tested. Consider the case of the majority of council tenants paying rents at or below average level. The standard amount included in their wage or positional benefit would cover their rent completely. They would need to claim no housing costs allowance at all. The housing costs allowance would be payable if someone had housing costs well above average. For example, a single woman who lives in a two-bedroom flat pays rent of £25 per week. She works full-time and earns just over the minimum wage. So she is able to pay the standard amount (say, £15 per week) out of her wages. She will therefore receive a net weekly housing costs allowance equal to a proportion of the £10 excess.

In practice, because the housing costs allowance is taxable, the level of the allowance would have to take account of basic rate tax. If, for example, a person needed a net payment of £8, they would be paid £10 gross (assuming basic rate tax of 20 per cent). The advantage of this apparently complicated mechanism is that it would allow a proportion of the housing costs allowance to be clawed back from higher-rate taxpayers. For example a 70 per cent rate taxpayer would only get a net payment of £3 in this situation. Like other benefits, housing cost allowance would be assessed on an individual basis.

Adults sharing accommodation would be considered liable for an equal part of the total joint housing costs. The variable housing cost allowance for someone sharing accommodation (for example, with a spouse) would be based on a proportion of their share of the housing costs in excess of the standard amount. In the vast majority of cases this would reduce the variable allowance to a small amount paid only to a minority of people. Suppose the woman in the above example stays in the same flat and a friend moves in with her. The friend is unemployed and receiving benefit. Both of them are expected to pay up to £15 per week in rent before claiming housing costs allowance. As this exceeds their actual rent share (£12.50 each), no allowance would be payable. Children could be taken into account on a proportionate basis, contributing the relevant amount of child benefit to the total rent.

Similar arguments about the need for the control of rents and for some sort of housing costs allowance apply for people renting privately. In the private sector, rent control and security of tenure must be strengthened. There is no excuse for the excessive profits gathered by many landlords at the expense of tenants and the state (via benefit payments). There should be an effective system of fixing and enforcing maximum rents. Private sector rents should be based on local authority rents wherever possible. In the case of luxury accommodation it would be very difficult to control the private market and there is no comparison with public sector housing. All private tenants need to be protected by proper security of tenure and enforcement of minimum standards of space, facilities and management. Support for privately-rented housing beyond reasonable rent allowances could be paid directly to selected landlords for improvements, repairs and maintenance repayable from the proceeds of sale of the property. Again, this would be shifting the burden of selectivity away from claimants; it would be the *owners* of property who were required to apply for special help. The principle is the same as that underlying our proposal for a subsidy payable to selected employers unable to pay the minimum wage (see Chapter 3).

It is sometimes argued that payment of HB can increase prices and encourage people to seek more expensive and luxurious accommodation; this is often called the 'up-marketing' problem. The likely extent of this problem should not be overstated. But the housing costs allowance system must incorporate some means of dealing with it. This could be achieved if the housing costs allowance were variable in such a way that it increased as rent increased up to a maximum, after which point it *decreased*, eventually to nothing. So that at a particular level the occupier would receive no housing costs allowance at all (other than the standard amount in their positional benefit or wages). This would work on the assumption that, beyond a certain level, the increase in a person's housing costs would be no longer related to need but would instead be a matter of choice and should therefore become the individual's responsibility.

This mechanism would have to be accompanied by a duty on local authorities to house people at reasonable rents. Such an extension of the Homeless Persons Act to include all homeless people (which is Labour Party policy) should also be accompanied by a duty on housing and health authorities to provide the necessary caring arrangements for people whose needs go beyond a lack of accommodation. Duties under an extended Homeless Persons Act would have to include provision of temporary accommodation, if necessary, at a reasonable cost. This would make the present unsatisfactory arrangements for board and lodging payments unnecessary. The government is restricting payment of board and lodging allowances, without doing anything to meet the need for housing or care for single people, disabled people or the elderly. These cuts will have a terrible consequence for those dependent on board and lodging.[19]

Spending on owner-occupation totally fails to meet socialist housing expenditure objectives. In this sector, the problem is not one of insufficient money, but that the spending produces high house prices and high profits for those who can take advantage of the concessions. Little or no new housing is produced and indeed an interest in maintaining the housing shortage is created, in order to increase house prices. The capital value of owner-occupied housing should be taxed when individuals make a profit from it, like other forms of wealth. Mortgage interest tax relief for high-rate taxpayers, however, could be ended immediately. This would limit the anomaly whereby the wealthiest receive the greatest proportionate relief and it would raise £200 million in extra tax in a full year.

The immediate abolition of mortgage interest tax relief for other borrowers, MIRAS, would be politically impossible and unjust — most people's existing commitments to mortgage repayments are not easily changeable, so many would suffer both through increased repayments and a decrease in the market value of their home. However, we have already argued that this relief should properly be called a subsidy on interest rates and it would be justifiable to take immediate measures to bring it under strict control.

The first step would be to cease calling it tax relief, which obscures the true nature of MIRAS, and identify it as a cash subsidy enabling lenders to charge lower interest rates for house purchase. The next stage in this policy would be to bring the total amount of subsidy under explicit budgetary control. One proposal for achieving this is to impose a cash limit on the total subsidy, the real value of which could be progressively reduced. Another proposal is that it could be reduced in line with falls in the market interest rate so that the government, rather than individual borrowers, benefited from the lower rates — by paying less subsidy — but borrowers would experience no change in their net payments. [20] At the same time the government could target the subsidy on those most in need. For example, it could be restricted to a single period of twenty or twenty-five years. People could not then extend tax relief indefinitely as they 'trade up' into larger and more expensive homes. Also the maximum mortgage eligible for tax relief could immediately be reduced to about £20,000, which is roughly equal to the average mortgage. Variations in the mortgage interest rates of between 10.25 per cent and 14 per cent in 1984/5 have caused changes in net repayments which are as great as the elimination of the subsidy altogether. These changes we propose would have a much smaller immediate effect on borrowers.

A socialist government could intervene in several ways to control house prices: it could increase the supply of owner-occupied housing (by building or making land available to other developers); the greater availability of public sector housing would depress private sector prices; and a tax such as capital transfer or stamp duty (or both) would discourage high prices.

The proposal for a housing costs allowance is straightforward for people renting accommodation, either public or private. Their housing costs are their rent. Payments to owner-occupiers present a problem: what are the equivalent costs of owner occupation? It would be unfair for the state to help owner-occupiers acquire an asset which maintains or increases its value. Equally it would be unjust to make owner-occupiers homeless when they were not in work or had a low wage. We propose, therefore, that owner-occupiers would be eligible for the housing costs allowance described above, but with two quali-fications. First, their housing costs might be considered to be equal to their actual repayments plus a fixed sum for maintenance and insurance. Secondly, housing allowance for repayments would in effect be a loan. The local author-ity would acquire a share in the home in return for paying the mortgage. This proportion could be repurchased at a later date. An owner would not need to claim housing costs allowance for the total amount of their repayments. If they wished, they could renegotiate their loan with the bank or building society to defer some part of the payments; building societies might have to be put under a duty to renegotiate. This arrangement for paying owner-occupiers' housing costs would depend on limiting the many tax privileges they currently enjoy. Some owner-occupiers would receive help with their housing costs from both interest subsidy and housing allowance during a transitional period.

These provisions could be accompanied by a 'right to rent' for owner-occupiers. An owner-occupier unable or unwilling to remain an owner could have the right to sell their home to a local authority. The local authority would be obliged to buy at its market value and then rent it, or a more suitable home, to the ex-owner. Elderly people in particular could be relieved of the anxiety and cost of repairs and maintenance, more housing would be preserved in a bet-ter state of repair, and councils would acquire an increasingly varied and dis-persed stock of housing. [21]

The variety of roles in housing that we have discussed above, including administration of the housing costs allowance, could be undertaken by local authorities — with progress to greater devolution. The current problems with housing benefit are partly a consequence of poor administration by some local authorities and in part the inherent confusion, complexity and meanness of the scheme. On balance, it would be a mistake to respond to these problems by proposing the transfer of HB administration back to central government. Our preference is for more local administration, accountability and policy-making power. However, local administration of housing costs allowances, etc. (as of all income maintenance benefits) must be subject to clear and enforceable statutory requirements. These must be strong enough to deal with those local authorities which for political reasons are unsympathetic to claimants. The legislation should set out minimum standards for administration, rights of appeal to independent bodies, effective means of redress and penalties on the local authority for breaches of its obligations.

Much else is wrong with housing apart from its finance. These proposals should create a framework in which those other problems of supply, manage-ment, control, accessibility, standards and so forth can begin to be resolved. All our proposals are intended to achieve four ends within the context of a socialist policy of income maintenance. First of all, to clearly separate expenditure on housing investment from income maintenance payments related to individuals' housing costs. Secondly, to concentrate expenditure in ways which increase the supply of good-quality housing. Thirdly, to limit its cost to a level that most people can afford. Finally, to ensure through income maintenance that all people can afford the housing they require.

Notes

1. The Association of Metropolitan Authorities' (AMA) Submission *Inquiry into British Housing*, London 1984.

2. *General Household Survey 1971*, Tables 5.46–8, *Inquiry into British Housing*, The AMA Submission, 1984; GLC Survey of Private Tenants in London, 1985; and Colin Brown, *Black and White Britain: The Third Policy Studies Institute Survey*, London 1984.

3. The Housing Programme 1965-1970.

4. By all public expenditure on local authority housing we mean the sum of the exchequer and rate fund contributions to local authority housing revenue accounts.

5. SHAC, *Bed and Breakfast: Policy Paper*, London 1985.

6. Several accounts have been written about the chaotic and harmful introduction of the HB scheme in 1982/3 (for example, SHAC, *The Cost of Chaos*, London 1984; CPAG, *Nobody's Benefit: A Survey of the Housing Benefit Scheme*, London 1984).

7. A smaller sum, £2.35, is deducted if the non-dependant is a pensioner or claiming SB and a further £2.20 is deducted for rates.

8. Owner-occupiers also pay no tax on the benefit in kind they receive by owning a house, that is, the right to live there rent-free (estimated to total £1,885 million in lost tax per year in 1982/3). This is called relief on imputed rental income and prior to 1963 was subject to tax. However, we do not consider it to be a concession to owner occupation along with mortgage interest and capital tax reliefs. We treat house purchase as consumption, rather than investment. First, because that is how most people treat it in practice; and, secondly, because treating house purchase as investment encourages house *buying* for speculative reasons as opposed to house *construction*, that is, it is partly a political choice rather than an abstract definition. For further discussion, see, for example, Matthew Warburton, *Housing Finance: The Case for Reform*, SHAC London 1983; and Goss and Lansley, *What Price Housing?* (revised) SHAC London 1984.

9. Labour Housing Group, *Right to a Home*, Nottingham 1984, p.86.

10. *Government Expenditure Plans 1985/6 to 1987/8*, Cmnd 9428, London 1984, p.23.

11. Ibid., p.111.

12. *Community Care*, 17 January 1985.

13. *National Dwelling and Household Survey*, London 1978, Table 8.

14. For further discussion of this issue see, for example, SHAC *Bed and Breakfast*.

15. These figures are not directly comparable, because definitions have changed during this period. Nevertheless it is true that the private rented sector has been declining throughout the late 1970s and early 1980s at the rate of 2 per cent per year.

16. *Guardian*, 9 February 1985, and GLC, *Going ... Going ... Almost Gone: What Price the Private Sector?*, London 1984.

17. J.A. Kay and M.A. King, *The British Tax System*, Oxford 1983.

18. Letter to *The Times* from the Royal Town Planning Institute, 2 January 1985; *Inquiry into British Housing*, The AMA submission; and SHAC, *Bed and Breakfast*.

19. SHAC, *Bed and Breakfast*.

20. We are grateful to Matthew Warburton for suggesting this approach to mortgage interest tax reform.

21. These ideas are drawn from Tim Daniel, 'A Better Deal for Home Owners' in Labour Housing Group, *Right to a Home*, Nottingham 1984.

8

Taxation and Benefits

Who *likes* paying tax? The returns on paying tax often don't appear to be worth it — long hospital waiting lists, complicated and inadequate benefits and a lot of weaponry. The tax system itself is widely believed to be unfair: some people don't pay 'their fair share' of tax, while others pay too much. Income tax has been levied at lower and lower incomes ever since it was first introduced and it is now exceptional for a working person *not* to pay tax, whereas for many years income tax was restricted to those with earnings at or above average. The tax burden falls disproportionately on low-income earners, yet the United Kingdom overall is not a heavily taxed nation.[1] Overcoming hostility to taxation relies on making it fair and on making the purpose of collecting it clearer. When the link between taxation and services is made apparent, support for tax is more forthcoming. A Gallup poll in 1983 revealed that 50 per cent of those interviewed wanted extended services and only 17 per cent preferred tax cuts. The Breadline Britain survey found that three-quarters of those interviewed would support an increase in income tax of a penny in the pound to enable everyone to afford necessities.[2]

The way in which taxation is publicly discussed tends to focus on this issue of what the state does or doesn't 'take away'. For example, a penny in the pound cut in tax which forced a cut of over £2 per week in pensions would be called 'generous'. Pensioners, however, wouldn't experience this generosity. The important issue is: *who* gets less money to spend as a result of the budget and *who* gets more? Who benefits from changes in taxation and social security? How does the tax system overall *transfer* money from some groups to others?

There is a crucial difference between government spending which uses up labour, capital or materials — called 'resource spending' — and government spending which simply 'transfers' spending power to other individuals. All social security expenditure is transfer spending; the government transfers money from some groups of individuals to others. The recipient of the money, not the government, spends it to consume resources. This is in contrast to government expenditure on the health services, teaching and armaments which is resource spending (this doesn't make it less desirable, just different).[3] For example, child benefit of £6.85 is paid to parents in respect of each child they are responsible for. The Tories like to point out how much this adds to government spending (about £4.5 thousand million). They treat it as a cost. In fact it illustrates well the idea of a transfer payment: money is collected in taxes and then distributed to those with children. Before 1978 state assistance with the cost of raising children was in the form of tax allowances: people with children paid less tax than those on similar incomes without children. This never figured as a government expenditure, as it was a reduction in tax rather than a benefit payment. So according to the Tories, assistance to parents didn't cost anything before 1978, whereas after that administrative change it suddenly cost many billions. This is ludicrous. Both child tax allowance and child benefit have the effect of transferring money to parents.

Taxation is relevant to income maintenance for the following reasons: firstly, it may reduce the disposable incomes of some people with low earnings and may result in their having an inadequate income; secondly, it is the means of raising revenue for redistribution in the income maintenance system; and, thirdly, taxation and benefits interrelate — many claimants pay tax and some benefits are taxable. The focus of this discussion therefore is personal taxation — that is, income tax, National Insurance contributions (NIC), wealth taxes and indirect taxes, for example, VAT — and its relation to social security. We also review the administrative impact of our proposals for benefit and taxation reform. This chapter is not a critique of the whole tax structure; extensive reforms of taxation are required in addition to those we propose.

The Tax System Today

How the Tax System Works

Tax is assessed relative to total income for one year, but most people pay it weekly or monthly — this is called Pay As Your Earn (PAYE). Generally husbands and wives are treated as one for tax purposes. They can elect for separate assessment, but this is only financially advantageous to high-income earners.[4]

Everyone is able to earn a fixed amount before paying tax; this is called the personal allowance and in 1985/6 it is £2,205 per year. A married man is allowed a larger amount of tax-free income, £3,455 per year, known as the married man's allowance (MMA), apparently on the assumption that he supports his wife. Single parents are eligible for an additional personal allowance equal to the MMA. There are other personal allowances, for example, the age allowance.

In addition to personal allowances, the British tax system offers a wide variety of reliefs. Certain categories of spending and saving are not liable to tax. The total amount not exempt is called taxable income.

Tax rates increase unevenly as income increases. Higher rates of tax only apply to income earned within the relevant *tax band*. For example, a person with an income just about average, say, £10,000, and mortgage interest payments of £1,000 would pay standard rate tax. The first £3,205 of their income is not liable for tax, so their taxable income is £6,795. Tax is paid at a rate of 30 per cent on this, making total tax due of £2,038.50. However, the principles of the system are best illustrated by considering someone on a very high income, paying some tax at the highest rate (as we refer to it several times, we shall call this the 'higher rate example' — less than 0.5 per cent of taxpayers actually fall into this category).[5] Let us take the example of a single person who earns £50,000 (about four times average earnings) and who has tax reliefs totalling £7,000. As their tax calculation is rather complicated it is set out in Table 8.1. Such a person would describe themselves as a '60 per cent rate taxpayer', even though less than £600 of their £50,000 income would be taxed at that rate.

Table 8.1

Income Band £	Tax rate %	Tax due £	Width of band £
0–9,205	0	0	9,205
9,206–25,405	30	4,860	16,200
25,406–28,405	40	1,200	3,000
28,406–33,605	45	2,340	5,200
33,606–41,505	50	3,950	7,900
41,506–49,405	55	4,345	7,900
49,406–50,000	60	357	595
TOTAL TAX DUE		17,052	
Average tax rate	34		

Earners pay National Insurance contributions (NIC) on all incomes up to £265 per week. Changes introduced in the 1985 budget for implementation in October 1985 make the structure of NIC more complex, allegedly to decrease the cost to employers of employing low-paid workers (and therefore to create more low-paid jobs). Like income tax, the rate of NIC increases as income increases, but, unlike tax, the higher marginal rate of NIC applies to *all* income not just to income within that band. Table 8.2 shows how NIC work. Employees covered by private pension schemes who are 'contracted out' of the state scheme pay 2.15 per cent less NIC at all income levels.

Table 8.2

Weekly income band £	NIC rate %	NIC payment due £
0–35.50	0	0
35.51–55	5	1.78–2.75
55–90	7	3.85–6.30
90–265	9	8.10–23.85
265+	0	23.85

Taxes on Income

There are two ways of assessing an individual's tax position. One measure is the *marginal rate* of tax, which is the rate of 'tax' — income tax and NI — payable on the next pound earned. The higher-rate taxpayer with a £50,000 income pays tax at a marginal rate of 60 per cent. The second measure is the total of income tax and NIC as a proportion of all income: the *average rate* of tax. The average rate of tax in the higher rate example is only about 36.5 per cent (including NIC). The average rate of tax is affected by the personal allowances, the tax bands and any other exemptions. From the government's point of view in raising revenue, it is the average rate that is important, because that relates to total tax paid to government. For those on average incomes, the average rate of income tax after exemptions, but excluding NIC, is currently about 18.5 per cent. So including NIC the average rate is between 25 per cent and 27.5 per cent.[6] The majority of taxpayers have a marginal rate of 39 per cent (30 per cent income tax plus 9 per cent NIC).

There are very extensive exemptions to income tax. The main categories of allowances and reliefs are listed in Table 8.3. These reliefs and allowances are undesirable for a number of reasons. They reduce the total amount of taxable income, the 'tax base'. The proportion of total income liable to income tax is estimated to be only 47 per cent after all exemptions are taken into account, and on average only about 16 per cent of all household income is paid in income tax. The total government revenue from income tax is £35.2 thousand million (25.5 per cent of government revenue).[7] As a consequence of the smaller tax base, marginal rates of tax have to be much higher than they would otherwise need to be to raise the same amount of revenue. For example, the initial rate of tax and NIC (35 per cent rising rapidly to 39 per cent) is much higher than in any other country in Europe or the United States.[8] Tax expenditure on these exemptions is often justified on the assumption that they will generate and support new economic activity. There is little evidence of this. In the case of housing, for example, we have argued that mortgage interest tax relief has primarily increased house prices and has not made houses more readily available.

Table 8.3

Type of exemption	Estimated tax loss £ million
Allowances:	
Single person's allowance	9,580
Married man's allowance	11,700
Age allowance	420
One-parent family allowance	140
Reliefs:	
Pension schemes	900–5,100[a]
(mainly contributions to pension funds)	
Self-employed retirement annuity	500
Life assurance premiums	725
(those started before April 1984)	
Mortgage interest relief	3,500
Interest on national savings	440
Income of charities	270
Government securities with foreign owner	300
Work expenses	275
Statutory redundancy pay	175

Note: [a] This figure varies dramatically depending on the assumptions made. For a discussion on this point see Chapter 5.
Source: *Government Expenditure Plans 1985/6*, Cmnd 9428.

Generally tax exemptions are arbitrary and uncontrolled in their economic effect. Tax exemptions favour the rich. In the higher rate example, a mortgage interest exemption of £3,000 reduces the tax paid at the 60 per cent rate, saving this person £1,800. Most people paying 30 per cent tax would gain only £900. Exemptions take effect at the highest marginal rate relevant to an individual taxpayer, and moreover they apply predominantly to the activities of rich people. This is just as true of personal allowances as it is of tax reliefs. The 1985 budget increased personal allowances by twice the rate of inflation, and it was claimed that this would help people on low pay. However, it helped the rich most. A person paying tax at the standard rate 'gained' £60 from the £200 increase in the personal allowance (they 'lost' money as a result of other tax changes). Someone paying tax at the highest rate gained £120 (they also gained substantially from other changes in the budget).

Finally, tax exemptions are the stuff of which tax avoidance is made. Many employers exploit exemptions to pay their higher-paid executives in ways which attract no tax or tax at a lower rate — through 'fringe benefits'. The UK is exceptional in the total value of fringe benefits employers give relative to employees' basic salaries. Fringe benefits are of advantage almost exclusively to people paying higher rates of tax and therefore further extend the inequalities of income distribution.[9] Tax exemptions also promote avoidance schemes like those exploited by the Rossminster company or the Vestey family's 'trusts' which have saved spectacular amounts in tax. The consequence of all these exemptions is that the richer person has more money and the state has less income.

NIC are calculated as a percentage on all earnings. So, when an increase in your weekly income takes you into one of the higher NIC bands, you have to pay a sudden increase in NIC: £1.77 at £35.50, £1.10 at £55 and £1.80 at £90. This can mean a loss in take-home pay. In relation to average weekly earnings £35.50 is a small amount of money, but this problem does affect a large number of part-time workers, almost exclusively women. At the other end of the scale — the upper earnings limit — NIC cease to be payable on any part of an income above £265 per week, which is less than the level at which a higher tax rate applies. Hence richer people pay a lower proportion of their total income on NIC than do those less well off. NIC is a tax and as a tax it is grossly unfair. It raises £24.6 thousand million in revenue for the government (17.8 per cent of all revenue).

For a discussion of the income maintenance effects of taxation, the taxation of benefits is clearly an important issue. At present some benefits are liable to tax (for example, unemployment benefit and retirement pensions); others are non-taxable (for example, child benefit and attendance allowance); and others have been reduced by 5 per cent in lieu of tax (for example, sickness benefit). Benefits have been made liable to tax without any compensatory increase in the level of benefit, which has meant a net loss of income for some claimants. It has been government policy to bring as many benefits as possible into tax in order to cut expenditure; it has considered taxing child benefit as a means of saving money.

For income maintenance policy, the other important effect of taxation is the extent to which it results in a redistribution of income. It is widely, but mistakenly, believed that the tax system is progressive in this sense. The income share of the richest 10 per cent was reduced from about 30 per cent to 28 per cent in 1980/81 and the income share of the 10 per cent of people on the lowest measurable incomes increased from about 3.5 per cent to 4.2 per cent after tax. This sort of distribution has remained largely unchanged for the past fifteen years. If benefit payments are taken into account as well, the entire taxation/benefits system appears to be a little more redistributive, particularly for those least well off. Whereas the lowest fifth of households shared less than 1 per cent of all income before tax and benefits were taken into account in 1981, they received about 7 per cent of 'final' income. The income share of the richest fifth was reduced from 46.4 per cent to 38.6 per cent by this process.

A substantial proportion of the population have very high incomes. Over 1.5 million people have incomes above twice average earnings and the incomes of the top 10 per cent account for over 27 per cent of the total national income. Therefore there is considerable income available for redistribution in a comprehensive income maintenance system. However, it would be naive to believe that a comprehensive redistribution of incomes would only affect the very rich. Current taxation has such little effect on incomes above the average that a comprehensive change would have to reduce the income share of the top 40 per cent of income earners — who have almost three-quarters of all pre-tax income. The distribution of incomes is densely bunched around and below the average; 62 per cent of all tax units have incomes between two-thirds and one and a half times average earnings. This puts a constraint on the extent to which income tax could change for people on income near the average.[10]

Taking advantage of popular hostility to taxation, Tory policy has been to intensify the inequalities we described above under the smokescreen of promised tax cuts. In fact basic rate tax payers on average income now pay more tax. The Tory government increased NIC, from 6.5 per cent to 9 per cent and have increased standard rate VAT from 8 per cent to 15 per cent. The reduction in the basic rate of tax was more than offset by both of these increases and the abolition of a lower tax rate (25 per cent) on the first £750 of income. As a consequence it was estimated that the burden of tax for those on two-thirds average earnings had increased from 27.7 per cent to 29.5 per cent of total income between 1979 and 1984. For a couple with children, the rise in their tax burden was equivalent to 9p on income tax. Tax cuts have mostly gone to those with the highest incomes. The 1979 budget cut the maximum rate of tax on earned income from 83 per cent to 60 per cent. About 154,000 'tax units' with high incomes gained an annual total of £1.5 thousand million in reduced tax (the same amount by which the social security budget was cut that year). The government has also extended some exemptions, such as mortgage interest tax relief. As a result of all these changes, by 1984 only families earning more than £34,145 per year were paying less tax than in 1979.

Wealth

Research has shown that rich people derived most of their wealth from inheritance. The principal reason for taxing wealth is to reduce the substantial inequalities which result. The second major argument relates to fairness. Unless there is a comprehensive taxation of income and wealth, people will try to avoid income tax by converting income into wealth.[11] There are currently two principal wealth taxes: taxation when money is passed from one person to another, capital transfer tax (CTT); and taxation as wealth accumulates, capital gains tax (CGT). Geoffrey Howe, when Chancellor, cursed capital taxes as 'capricious, savage and oppressive' and in his 1980 and 1981 budgets introduced the exemptions to CTT and CGT which virtually abolished these as effective taxes and have made them into tax avoidance measures for the rich. But Tory claims that wealth taxation inhibits the entrepreneurial flair of small business people accumulating capital to pass on to their children is not supported by the conclusions of detailed research.[12] The yield from both these taxes was already small before 1979 and is now derisory — only £1.9 thousand millions, or 1.4 per cent of all tax revenue.

CTT (previously estate duty) applies to gifts and bequests. Unlike income tax, it is not levied on what people earn or accumulate. It is a tax on transfers of wealth, during a person's lifetime as well as at death. But it is so riddled with exceptions and exemptions that it is relatively easy to avoid. The Tory budget of 1981 reduced the yield from CTT almost to the point of abolition.[13] In any ten-year period a couple who are taxed independently for CTT can give to their children a total of £194,000 and not pay a penny in tax. Both the marginal and the average rates of tax on transfers of capital are much lower than income tax and bear no relation whatsoever to the income of either the donor or the recipient.

CGT is paid on the increased value of assets such as shares, bank deposits or property investments when their cash value is realized — usually when they are sold. Like CTT there are many exemptions which massively reduce its yield. In one sense it is similar to an income tax: it taxes the money 'earned' by the increasing value of assets. CGT is a pretty poor income tax — it is only levied at a basic rate of 30 per cent. This shows why it is so advantageous for higher-rate income tax payers to turn income into a capital gain if at all possible — they can save up to 30p in the pound. Although CGT was introduced to reduce opportunities for tax avoidance, it has evolved into an officially sanctioned avoidance scheme.[14]

The revenue from VAT was more than doubled by the government in 1979 when the rate was put up from 8 per cent to 15 per cent and it now stands at £18.3 thousand million (13.3 per cent of total government revenue). VAT takes a greater proportion of the incomes of the least well off than the rich.[15] Its advantage to the government is that this process is concealed. It is clear exactly how much tax you pay when it is written on your wage slip. It's not so clear when it adds 15p to a portion of fish and chips, 1.5p to a Mars bar, £3.80 to a coat or £22 to a home computer. Increases in VAT have enabled the Tories to claim that tax has been cut, whereas most people have simply paid a little less income tax but much more NIC and VAT.

Proposals for Change

Unified Tax and Benefit Systems

Earlier in this chapter we identified problems caused by the reduction of the tax base by reliefs and allowances. We discussed how this forced the income tax system to have a high marginal rate of tax in order to generate sufficient revenue for government spending and transfer payments. In earlier chapters we referred to another problem concerning high marginal rates of tax — the poverty trap. This can be described as a high marginal rate of benefit withdrawal/tax for people on low incomes. For example, the combined effect of income tax, NIC and HB is a marginal rate of benefit withdrawal/tax of 77 per cent.

Schemes for the unification of the tax and benefits systems which we discussed in chapters 2 and 3, such as those proposed by the Alliance parties and the Institute of Fiscal Studies, are often presented as a solution to this anomaly. In order to eliminate the extreme examples where benefit withdrawal/tax is over 100 per cent, they propose combining the administration of tax and benefits. Most of these proposals openly consolidate a very high marginal rate of benefit withdrawal/tax on low incomes — under these schemes there would be a means test on benefit payments. Thus, for example, the IFS scheme proposes that benefit should be withdrawn from a low-paid worker with children at a rate of 89p in the pound. The Social Democratic Party version proposes a total marginal rate of 84 per cent for a couple with children.[16]

Some of those who put forward the idea of a social credit or basic income guarantee (BIG) (see Chapter 3) claim that this is the best way of getting rid of means-testing. We have already criticized such proposals on political grounds. Worse still, the structure of social credit schemes is such that the elimination of means-testing is made more difficult. In these schemes every adult gets the social credit irrespective of their other income. Also everyone pays tax on all earnings. Benefit payment and tax liability would be calculated in the following way. Someone with low earnings would pay less in tax on those earnings than they received from the state. As earnings increase, there comes a point at which the tax payment equals the social credit; this is usually called the 'break-even point'. The break-even point plays the same role in this taxation system as a personal allowance does in the present one, that is, people only start paying net tax when their income exceeds the break-even point. The higher the break-even point, the smaller the tax base (as for higher personal allowances) and, consequently, higher marginal tax rates are necessary. With an income above that level, their tax payment would exceed their social credit. In practice, the administration of tax collection and social credit payment could be combined, so that people received a net social credit (with tax liability deducted from it) or paid net tax (with social credit deducted from it).

In order for this scheme to work, two restrictive conditions have to be met. The first is that the social credit must be sufficiently *high* to keep people alive and well. Secondly, in order to raise sufficient revenue to pay for the social credit, the break-even point has to be sufficiently *low* to ensure that a large proportion of income is taxable. These two constraints are in conflict. The effect of these two constraints is that there has to be a narrow gap between the level of the social credit and the break-even point. The whole social credit has to be withdrawn as a person's income rises from the credit level to the break-even point. So narrowing the gap between these amounts means that the marginal rate of benefit withdrawal/tax on incomes between these levels, that is, on *low* incomes, has to be very high.

This need for a high marginal rate applies only to incomes below the break-even point. Once a person's income is above this level there is no necessity to retain the same high marginal rate (apart from the overall need to raise revenue). Consequently it is very improbable in practice that the high marginal rate applying to people with incomes below the break-even point would also be applied to people with higher incomes. Inevitably the high rate would be restricted to those on whom it is structurally necessary — all those receiving a net benefit payment. In other words, there would be a means test. The only other way to achieve a low break-even point is to reduce the level of the social credit to a point below subsistence. In this case, people relying solely on the social credit would have to receive a means-tested top-up payment. In practice, any social credit scheme inevitably relies on a means test.

The only way to overcome these problems is to ensure that everyone in work receives a minimum wage which doesn't need to be topped up by a means-tested benefit. Paying a minimum wage enables the link between the minimum income and the break-even point to be cut. It is even possible to levy tax on the minimum wage itself so long as people are left with an adequate income after tax. In terms of the discussion above, the break-even point can be at any level sufficient to generate the required revenue. It can be at, above or even below the minimum wage level. A minimum wage would enable all earnings (that is, 69 per cent of all household income) to be brought into tax, permitting much greater fairness in the structure of income tax. In contrast, a social credit scheme automatically reduces the tax base because the level of the credit determines both the benefit level and the level of the tax allowance — the higher the benefit, the higher the allowance and the smaller the tax base. A system with a minimum wage, however, enables the tax base to be widened because tax allowances would not be needed to support the low paid.

Comprehensive Reform

The principles underlying the present taxation system conflict with the objectives of a socialist approach to income maintenance. Overall, the tax/benefits system is redistributive to only a very limited degree; it discriminates against women; and couples are generally treated as single units for assessment. The discussion of taxation in the first part of this chapter also identified technical problems with the tax/benefits system. The excessive use of exemptions significantly reduces the tax base and forces marginal rates to be high; the system is not consistently progressive; and the separation of income and wealth taxation under differing systems favours avoidance. Furthermore, the largely unplanned interrelation of the tax and benefits system is both hard to comprehend and results in unacceptably high marginal rates of benefit withdrawal/tax for low-paid workers.

Elsewhere in this book we have reviewed the arguments in favour of scrapping many tax reliefs. In Chapter 5 we proposed the full taxation of all pensions including lump-sum payments and in Chapter 7 we proposed the phased abolition of mortgage interest tax relief. The abolition of other reliefs would generate a further £1.5 thousand million additional tax revenue at current tax rates.[17]

Many people who accept the desirability of abolishing tax reliefs would put allowances into a different category. Indeed it is often argued that allowances should be maintained or even increased to protect the low paid from impoverishment caused by paying tax. However, this argument would entirely lose its force if all workers had sufficient income to pay tax. A statutory minimum wage plus separate assessment in the benefits system and adequate child support would ensure that even those on the lowest pay could afford to pay tax. People would have an adequate income not by being taken out of tax (and given benefits), but by receiving a reasonable wage in the first place.

Another argument used in favour of allowances is that taxing low incomes, some of which may be from benefits, involves the state in taking back money which it has handed out. The current mess of overlapping and contradictory benefits and taxation is in obvious need of reform. But we do not agree that there is anything inherently wrong in both paying tax and receiving benefits. The problems arise because benefits are means-tested and there is no coordination between the tax and benefits systems. Child benefit shows that the payment of benefit to taxpayers does not necessarily lead to messy administrative problems. It is not an issue of principle, but one of administration and of degree. In our proposals the extent of any overlap of wages and benefits would be largely overcome, because the minimum wage would ensure a sufficient income without the payment of means-tested benefits such as FIS and HB. If the purpose of allowances is to help the low paid, it is a very inefficient way of doing so. There are millions in work who remain in poverty and raising allowances would help the rich more than it would raise the incomes of the low paid. Moreover it would reduce the tax base still further.

The case for abolishing tax allowances is strong, but one further objection could be made: some tax allowances are specifically for taxpayers with dependants or with special needs. Making provision through the tax system for such people is inegalitarian: the assistance is denied those who pay no tax and, like all exemptions, benefits the rich most. It would be much fairer to meet needs through a system of separately assessed positional and cost-related benefits such as we have proposed. A minimum wage policy creates the possibility of a fairer and more comprehensive reform: abolishing personal allowances altogether and having a low initial rate of tax. So long as the minimum wage is set at a level which takes account of tax at this basic rate, then the incomes of benefit recipients and people on or near the minimum wage are secured. Such a system would permit a very fair and progressive tax structure, in which those on the lowest incomes pay the lowest marginal and average rates of tax and these rates would increase progressively. The muddle caused by the confused and unplanned interrelation between tax and benefits would be eliminated. If there were no tax allowances or reliefs, then the initial marginal rate of tax could be much lower. The idea of taxing benefits seems unpalatable, given their low levels at present, but in principle all the other objections to tax exemptions apply to the exemption of benefits from tax (an untaxed benefit is equivalent in the tax system to a tax exemption).

The taxation of all incomes has important political implications. Government ministers are actively considering proposals for a poll or residents tax which would impose a flat-rate levy on all those registered to vote. Some Tories have even implied that claimants getting full rebate on their rates should be deprived of their right to vote in local elections. If everyone paid income tax, then their citizenship and political rights could not be challenged in this pernicious way.

As far as possible, the taxation of wealth and income should be equivalent, so there is no advantage in treating income as wealth or vice versa. The first step in this would be to combine capital gains with income tax, so that a capital gain would be taxed in the same way as additional income, although some indexation of gains to take account of inflation would be necessary. Exemptions for small capital gains may need to be retained for administrative purposes. Similarly CTT could be strengthened by the abolition of exemptions for all but the smallest transfers and, like capital gains, transfers would be taxed at marginal rates related to income taxation. This would establish an effective means of taxing wealth. An alternative method of taxing transfers is an accessions tax. This extends the principle of the comprehensive taxation of incomes in all forms by taxing the recipient on the capital sum received. The taxation of capital gains realized by the sale of a house which had increased in value could be deferred if the money was used to purchase another home for occupation by the taxpayer. Transfer or accession of a home would always be taxable.

The extension of the principles of comprehensive income taxation to savings would lead to the following approaches. Saved income could be taxable, that is, contributions to savings institutions would be paid out of taxed income. Thereafter increases in the value and interest from the savings would also both be taxable as income. But the saver would not pay tax on withdrawals. An alternative approach, which would perhaps encourage a greater level of savings but would be equivalent in its overall tax effect, would be to allow contributions to savings institutions to be offset against income tax — in other words, saved income would be tax-free. However, all withdrawals, whether of the initial sum or interest and capital gain, would be liable for tax. In practice, this would mean that individuals deferred both the income and the tax payable on it. Either of these two approaches could be adapted to the taxation of pension funds. Unlike at present, no savings would be preferentially treated for tax purposes and all saved income would be liable for tax at some point.

So long as the level of benefits takes account of tax at the basic rate, people on low incomes would receive adequate incomes overall, and the only persuasive argument in favour of exempting benefits from tax falls away. Moreover in a scheme which proposes non-means-tested benefits, it is only fair that benefits paid to the better off are clawed back to a certain extent through tax. Therefore we propose that positional benefits should be taxable. Taxation of cost-related benefits would be more problematic. It is arguable that they should be non-taxable, as they are paid to compensate people for necessary expenditure on needs which give rise to additional costs. According to this argument, even better-off claimants with such additional needs should, after meeting those needs, be left in the same position as someone else with the same initial income but no such needs. So someone with a high salary and high housing costs could meet all their housing costs out of benefit and be no worse off than a similar person living in cheaper housing.

Another view is that cost-related benefits should be taxable. According to this view, the primary aim of cost-related benefits should be to ensure that people with extra needs causing additional expenditure should be able to meet those needs. This purpose is satisfied if cost-related benefits are taxable and are paid inclusive of tax at the basic rate. Another argument supporting the taxation of cost-related benefits is that some cost-related benefits relate to needs over which the claimant has a degree of control. This argument evidently does not apply to disability cost allowance, but arguably does apply to housing costs allowance. So long as people are able to meet necessary expenditure on these needs where there is an element of choice, it is fair to reclaim more of the benefit from higher-rate taxpayers. Once again, all the general arguments against allowances would apply to the exemption of cost-related benefits.

On balance, we favour the option of taxing cost-related benefits, so long as people on minimum income could never be lifted into a higher-rate tax band by their cost-related benefit alone.[18] If this latter approach were adopted, child benefit would be taxable, but the practical implications of taxing child benefit depend on how it is categorized. Child benefit could be treated as a positional benefit of the child (but paid on the child's behalf to the parent). In this case it would be taxable on the child's income, so in reality only children with an independent income would be affected. Alternatively, it could be treated as a cost-related benefit paid to the parent to meet the necessary extra costs of supporting a child. In this case it would be taxable income of the parent. On balance, we would suggest that child benefit be a taxable cost-related benefit of parents, so it would be clawed back in part from higher-rate taxpayers.

Administration

The aim of integrating the structure and principles of taxation and benefits in a comprehensive income maintenance system applies equally to administration. As far as is possible, payment of benefits and collection of taxes should be jointly administered. This would be simpler for everyone. It would also help to make the nature of benefits as transfer payments much clearer and it would emphasize the state's responsibility for planning incomes.

Efficient administration could be achieved if benefits were paid net of tax assuming a benefit-level income only. Tax could be deducted from earnings taking into account payment of benefit net of this minimum tax. For full-time workers this would be relatively straightforward. Part-time workers would need some mechanism whereby they could be assured of receiving *every week* the proper amount of benefit to cover the hours they did not work. If the total number of hours they worked were much the same each week, this would not be a problem. The tax/benefit office would know this pattern of work, could pay benefit appropriately and notify the employer of the correct rate of tax. If, however, the hours varied weekly, then the payment of benefit would have to be adjusted weekly to take account of that. For example, the minimum wage for part-time workers could be set in five-hourly bands. Anyone working between fifteen and twenty hours a week would have to be paid at least the minimum wage for twenty hours' work. They would then be eligible for fifteen hours worth of benefit (assuming the basic working week to be thirty-five hours).

A separate problem would apply to a few people on high part-time earnings which fluctuated: the total income for one week or month could take them into the next tax band. This problem would be minimized if the basic tax band was reasonably wide, at least up to the level of average earnings. This difficulty would be further reduced if assessment of benefit and earnings for part-time workers was calculated on bands of hours, rather than being variable by as little as one hour, as suggested above. Comprehensive computerization of taxation and benefits would also allow regular reviews of some part-time workers' tax, so that under- or over-payments could be recognized and adjusted for before they became too large.

Administration of tax and benefits is a serious problem with the present systems. Failures in administration predominantly affect the very people which the system is intended to assist — parents, low-paid, part-time and irregularly employed workers. So let us see how our system would work in practice.

(1) *Full-time Worker with no Taxable Benefit.* Such a person would see very little change in administration from the present. Her tax would be deducted by her employer relative to each week's or month's earnings. There would be a single tax table for all incomes.

(2) *Full-time Worker with Taxable Housing Costs Allowance.* His allowance would be paid with basic rate tax already deducted. Payment could be by some form of order book or girocheque. The tax/benefit office would give the employer a 'tax code' showing the weekly or monthly gross taxable benefit income. His employer would add his housing costs allowance to his earnings in order to calculate the appropriate tax band. However, in actually assessing tax due, the employer would take account of basic rate tax already paid on the housing costs allowance.

(3) *Disabled Part-time Worker.* She would be eligible for a positional benefit for those hours of the week that she wasn't in paid employment and a disablement cost allowance. She could choose how to pay tax. If she worked regular hours she could choose to pay tax and receive benefit as in (2) above. If she worked irregular hours and was concerned about overpaying or underpaying tax, she could choose to do the reverse process. She would receive her earnings from her employer net of tax appropriate for the week or month in which they were earned. With that she would also receive a statement of how many hours she had worked, earnings received and tax paid. The tax and benefits office would then calculate the benefit payable for the outstanding hours and make a payment net of tax, taking into account her earnings and tax paid for that period.

One approach to assessing the administrative effects of reforms would be to identify in the present income maintenance system the sources of administrative problems and of conflicts between officials and workers. These are the widespread use of means tests; aggregation of benefit and the associated cohabitation and liable relative rules; contribution tests; the complexity of benefit regulations; and the relations of power between claimants and officials in the assessment of benefits. Proponents of schemes such as benefit credits or negative income tax justify their proposals in terms of administrative simplification and yet they largely fail to address the experience of problems in the present system.

As a result, the schemes put forward perpetuate all the weaknesses of the present system identified above for example, means-testing, aggregation and elementary issues such as changes in circumstances. Furthermore, they attempt to gloss over the effects of these with appeals to the power of new technology. By contrast, our proposals are based on an experience of where the present system goes wrong and therefore are explicitly intended to overcome those problems by eliminating their fundamental causes.

Notes

1. *The Structure of Personal Income Taxation and Income Support*, Third Special Report from the Treasury and Civil Service Committee Session 1982/3, 11 May 1983, p.xi (widely known as the *Meacher Report*); and of the ten Common Market countries, Britain ranked sixth in terms of tax as a proportion of the total economy.

2. Also, 35 per cent said they would support a 5p in the pound increase, with an equal number opposed to this — see Joanna Mack and Stewart Lansley, *Poor Britain*, London 1985.

3. For a discussion of this distinction see Ian Gough, *The Political Economy of the Welfare State* p.80. London 1979.

4. A government discussion paper on tax was announced in the 1985 budget which would consider a restructuring of personal allowances to give everyone the same allowance and abolish MMA, although non-working married partners could still transfer their allowance to their spouse.

5. *Meacher Report*, p.xxii.

6. *Meacher Report: The Evidence* p.213. Note these figures refer to 'tax units'.

7. *Meacher Report*, p.lvii; and *Treasury Financial Statement and Budget Report 1985-86*, London 1985.

8. *Meacher Report*, p.xxxv.

9. A serious problem for a tax system is that expenses properly incurred whilst earning an income should be exempt from tax. Defining what those are has exercised the imaginations of tax officials and judges ever since income tax was introduced.

10. *Meacher Report*, p. lxxvi, using 1980 figures; *Meacher Report: The Evidence*, p.213; Frank Field, ed., *The Wealth Report No. 2*, London 1983 pp.38–9; and *Social Trends 1984*.

11. Discussion of wealth taxes requires at least a working definition of wealth. Assets that can be bought and sold — 'marketable assets' — are usually included in definitions of wealth: houses, land, company shares, life policies, other savings and bonds and government securities are all included in this definition. For figures see HMSO *A to Z of Income and Wealth* pp. 21, 24, 25, London 1979; *Wealth Report No. 2*, p. 13; *Social Trends 1984*, p.84; and J.A. Kay and M.A. King, *The British Tax System*, p.141-2 and 62. Oxford 1983.

12. J.A. Kay and M.A. King, p.158. Oxford 1983.

13. The already high exemption, below which no tax at all is paid, now applies to a ten-year period instead of a lifetime. Every ten years a rich person can give away £67,000 free of tax. In addition to this s/he can give away £3,000 a year tax-free.

14. For figures on the small yield of CGT see *Wealth Report*, p.29.

15. *Wealth Report*, p.67.

16. A.W. Dilnot, J.A. Kay and C.N. Morris, *The Reform of Social Security*, Oxford 1984; and Social Democratic Party *Attacking Poverty*, London 1983 p.10, table 2.

17. Some exemptions can not be withdrawn — for example, foreign holdings and work expenses — for practical or technical reasons. It is not possible to simply add these figures up and call it total increased tax revenue. Some people gain from several reliefs, the loss of which might bring them

into a higher tax band. On the other hand, some people might be reduced to an unacceptably low income and therefore require compensation. Changes to exemptions and rates of tax would complement one another, so that people would be less likely to be left with inadequate post-tax incomes.

18. One mechanism for achieving this would be for the threshold between the basic rate and other rates of tax to be equal to either: the sum of wages plus the cost-related benefit for any individual; or the ordinary threshold for other taxpayers, whichever is the higher.

9

Tory Reform or Socialist Radicalism?

Tory Reform

To socialists it has always seemed that there should be a natural alliance between the labour movement and claimants. Many claimants — for example, the elderly, the disabled, single parents, the unemployed, the sick — are themselves ex-trade unionists or trade unionists of the future. Conversely, many trade unionists are either claiming benefits already, as parents, tenants or ratepayers, or are the claimants of the future, when disabled or retired. What is more, the two groups seemed to share a common status as the dispossessed of the capitalist economy. The capitalist economic system hinges on the ownership of wealth and capital: workers and claimants have had neither. In the period of mass unemployment between the wars, claimants and workers combined to exert substantial political pressure on an unyielding state. The election of a Labour government and the creation of the welfare state after the Second World War seemed to bring this alliance of workers and claimants out of the cold and into the very institutions of the British state. The labour movement was apparently given a place in the decision-making of government — or, at least, a recognized negotiating position. And, almost as a precondition for the industrial and political truce, the principle of state responsibility for disadvantaged groups was embodied in the new social security system.

But the very characteristics of the new social security system which made it readily comprehensible to and popular among trade unionists prefigured the dissolution of the apparently natural alliance between workers and claimants. Beveridge's beloved insurance principle is essentially worker-based: paying benefits to those who have earned contributions and denying them to those

This chapter was added after the publication in June 1985 of the government's consultation paper: The Reform of Social Security.

who have not. Forty years on, the alliance which seemed to be so firmly entrenched is in disarray. The divisions between workers and the workless seem to be of even greater significance than the divisions between workers and the owners of capital. Among workers there are chronic divisions between the organized and the unorganized, home owners and tenants, those with pension rights and those without, full-time and part-time workers, men and women, blacks and whites, well paid and low paid. Moreover the present government feels able to move away from the principles of collective responsibility which were apparently agreed in the 1940s.

Few of the divisions which have grown up can be blamed exclusively on the income maintenance system. But the lack of attention from socialists to issues of principle in income maintenance has facilitated a tragic reversal for the left. Rather than being the cornerstone of a close alliance between trade unionists and the disadvantaged, social security has added its ample weight to the emphasis of divisions. A combination of earnings-related state pensions with state support for private occupational schemes preserves the division between the better and lower paid in retirement. National Insurance emphasizes the divisions between those in jobs and the non-employed. The use of the family unit as a basis of assessment and the overt discrimination against women reinforce conflicts of interest between men and women. The spread of 'internal controls' on black claimants feeds the potential for racism. Tax subsidies greet owner-occupiers while tenants are forced to pay more and more for worse and worse housing. The ever-growing use of means tests reproduces the traditional distinction between the 'respectable working class' and the poor. The income maintenance system supports millions in poverty and debt, while the extent of redistribution of income and wealth remains small. Far from being a radical break with post-war developments in social security, Norman Fowler's proposals for the reform of social security can be seen as a calculated attempt to exploit and intensify these divisions.

Fowler's Proposals

Norman Fowler's review of the structure of social security was concluded with the publication of 'The Reform of Social Security' in June 1985.[1] This consultative green paper set out the government's proposals and supporting arguments. If implemented, the proposals would consolidate the role of means-testing and leave hundreds of thousands of claimants significantly worse off. Nevertheless, to some extent, the presentation of the proposals reveals a failure of political nerve. This was dramatically revealed when, as the printing presses were about to turn, the government decided to remove figures from the text which would have indicated the levels of benefit and therefore the numbers of losers and the extent of cuts. Yet those parts of the 'consultation paper' which were considered safe for public consumption do express a very clear and detailed statement of the government's strategy for social security.

The principles for reform that the green paper sets out are the common themes of Tory policy: 'controlling expenditure' — ie cutting the social security budget; 'targetting benefits on those most in need' — ie consolidating means tests and cutting benefits for all but the very poor; 'simplifying complex and overlapping rules' — ie restricting rights to benefit and appealing to rough justice; 'increasing incentives to work' — ie cutting benefits paid to the unemployed; and 'enhancing individual responsibility and independence' — ie. cutting the rates of benefit and privatising benefits and services wherever possible.

One effect of the proposals would be to intensify the divisive nature of social security. The green paper presents those people whose main source of income is state social security as 'dependants' who are a burden on the rest of society. The overall aim is reduce their numbers as much as possible and divide them from the majority of the population who will be encouraged to secure their income through wages, family dependancy and private welfare. The replacement of the state earnings-related pension scheme (SERPS) with compulsory private pensions would differentiate still more clearly the economic and political interests of a poorly paid person eventually dependent on a basic state pension, from someone who is better off and has a substantial personal or occupational pension. Undermining insurance based and universal benefits paid to individuals, such as child benefit, has an indirect effect on relations between women and men: the means-tested benefits favoured by the government are generally assessed on a family basis and are paid to the 'breadwinner'. The introduction of a test of recent residence in the UK to the principal means-tested benefit would encourage and excuse more controls on black claimants and leave some with no money at all. Tenants and owner-occupiers on low incomes would suffer cuts totalling £500 million in lost housing benefit. Better-off owner-occupiers would continue to receive their £3,500 million subsidy.

Despite the general trend of the proposals, the government professes a commitment to the principle of collective responsibility for welfare through the national insurance system and child benefit. To support this claim they point to the retention of the basic state pension and child benefit. This 'commitment' rings hollow, for in the weeks following the green paper child benefit was cut by 5 per cent and basic pensions have been set on a course to fall steadily in value in relation to average earnings. Although this 'commitment' can in part be attributed to a failure of nerve, it is also based on the government's need to justify the national insurance 'tax' of 16.5 per cent (the second largest source of government revenue). Looked at more positively the government's caution can be seen as an expression of its fear of the deep-rooted popular support for non-means-tested benefits.

Before assessing the consequences of the green paper proposals in relation to the analysis developed in earlier chapters we summarise the main points. These proposals simply omit any reference whatsoever to the many people whose needs and circumstances the government is unwilling to address or whose needs are met inadequately by the present system — those who do not fit into easy categories.

SUPPLEMENTARY BENEFIT

Supplementary benefit (SB) would be renamed 'income support'. Weekly additions paid for special needs in the SB scheme would all be abolished, as would the long-term rate of benefit. Instead, the basic benefit would be topped up by 'premiums' — fixed weekly amounts paid to particular categories of claimant. The key categories would be: claimants with children; single parents; claimants aged sixty to seventy-nine; claimants aged over eighty; those aged sixty to seventy-nine who are seriously disabled or were chronically sick before they reached sixty; and those under the age of sixty who have serious disabilities or are chronically sick or whose spouses are seriously disabled. Childless unemployed claimants would receive no premiums. Unemployed young people under the age of twenty-five would be even worse off, eligible only for a reduced level of basic benefit. A 'presence test' would be introduced to prevent those who have recently arrived in this country from claiming benefit. The government also tentatively proposes to abolish or restrict the period of payment of mortgage interest to owner-occupiers on SB. SB claimants would also lose help with water rates.

SOCIAL FUND

SB single and urgent needs payments for items such as furniture, bedding, fuel or travel costs would be abolished. Instead claimants and the low paid would have to apply to a discretionary 'social fund'. Normally payment would be in the form of a loan, but in some circumstances grants could be made. The social fund, modelled on charity, would make a payment only after a deliberately subjective investigation into personal needs and circumstances. Unlike any benefit since the Poor Law the social fund would have a fixed annual budget, so help would simply cease if money ran out before the end of the financial year.

HOUSING BENEFIT

Norman Fowler has said that the proposed changes to housing benefit (HB) would result in cuts of around £500 million per year. The main cuts would be made by increasing the rate of withdrawal of HB applied to increases in family income. This 'taper' would only apply to net income rather than gross income as at present. Nearly all claimants would lose some money and between 1 and 1.8 million claimants would lose entitlement altogether. The government proposes that all claimants, even those getting SB, should cease to receive help with the first 20 per cent of their rates. Furthermore, the level of subsidy paid by central government to local authorities would be cut. The heating rebate paid to claimants on SB with high fixed heating charges or inefficient systems would also go. For the first time those with savings over £6,000 would be barred from getting HB at all.

FAMILY CREDIT

The government proposes to 'privatize' family income supplement — to be renamed 'family credit'. It would be paid in the wage packet instead of as a cash benefit from the DHSS. It would continue to be means-tested but awarded for only six months at a time rather than a year. The government proposes to transfer resources from the universal child benefit and one parent benefit into this new scheme. The five per cent cut in child benefit in November 1985 is the first step in this plan. The level of assistance and its calculation would be closely related to the income support scheme in such a way as to ensure that families out of work were always worse off than those in which at least one parent was in work. The provision of free school meals to children in families with low earnings would be stopped.

PENSIONS

The green paper focuses on the proposal to replace SERPS with compulsory private pensions. Those retiring before 2002 would still receive the same earnings-related pension. Those due to retire during the decade after that would receive a 'bonus' to the contributions they have already made to SERPS, but would lose the right to make further contributions to the scheme. Younger contributors would have the pension rights which they have already 'earned' preserved, with no further SERPS entitlement building up from April 1987. Employers and employees would be compelled to make combined contributions to private pension schemes equal to at least four per cent of earnings. Employers would only have to contribute half of this minimum; the rest would fall to employees. The 6.25 per cent rebate on national insurance contributions for employees contracted out of SERPS would be abolished. There would be a common rate of national insurance for all employees, apart from the low paid. The overall cost of national insurance and pension contributions combined would increase for all workers. The current requirement for pension funds to provide a guaranteed minimum pension would be abolished as would the government's commitment to top up occupational pensions to the SERPS level (although this is not made clear in the consultation paper).

The government also proposes that the retirement age could become more flexible — with a choice to retire an any age between sixty and seventy. However, those retiring early would receive a reduced pension and would have to convince the DHSS that they could support themselves without needing to claim means-tested benefits.

MATERNITY, DEATH AND WIDOWHOOD

Both the maternity and death grants would be replaced by help through the social fund. The rules governing the payment of maternity allowance would be altered to prevent women from claiming the allowance for two successive pregnancies without working in between. Widow's allowance would be abolished and replaced by a one-off grant of £1,000, and payment of widow's pension in full would be restricted to those qualifying after the age of fifty-five. This would result in cuts of over £100 million per year in widows' benefits.

The Reviews Reviewed

In this book we have argued for an analysis of income maintenance derived from an understanding of the needs and circumstances of people with inadequate incomes. The Tory proposals are concerned exclusively with the state's interests. How does the green paper look in the light of our earlier analysis?

THE UNEMPLOYED AND LOW PAID

The unemployed hardly appear in the government's discussions. For the government it is not the needs of the unemployed which are important, but rather the need to give them sufficient incentive to find work. We argued in chapter three that this creates a tension between the government's low wage strategy and social security. The only solution open to the government is to ensure that unemployment benefits are lower than the incomes of other claimants and those in work, however poorly paid. The unemployed person's rate of income support would be the lowest level and they would receive least help from the discretionary social fund. The consultation paper explains the relations between income support, child benefit and the family credit entirely in terms of work incentives — it would 'ensure that families are not worse off in work than unemployed'.[2] We also argued in chapter three that means-tested benefits paid to people with low earnings amount to a subsidy to employers who pay low wages. This aspect of social security would be made explicit in the new system because family credit would be paid in the wage packet. This means that employers would know by exactly how much low wages were supplemented by the state. Their position in wage negotiations would be further strengthened and wages could be further depressed in many industries. The green paper ignores the separate needs of people working part time and simply subsumes their needs in the more general problem of family poverty.

WOMEN, MEN AND CHILDREN

The government acknowledges in the green paper that claimants with children suffer some of the worst effects of poverty. However they come to the perverse conclusion that improvements in benefits for this group should be partly paid for by cuts in the level of child benefit. This would have the worst effect on those with incomes just above the government's chosen poverty line. This would also accentuate the differences in the standard of living between those with children and those without. Moreover, the switch of resources from child benefit to means-tested benefits would worsen the financial position of women with children as child support becomes increasingly restricted to the very poor. The change from family income supplement to family credit would in many cases mean a transfer of income from women to men within the family. Carers are nowhere considered to be a group in need of an independent income and the aggregation of assessment is assumed. Pressure on families would be further intensified by the payment of reduced benefit to people under twenty-five which would not allow them to maintain their own home.

PENSIONERS

The largest 'savings' in government spending will eventually accrue from the replacement of SERPS by compulsory private pensions. In chapter 5 we examined the government's difficulties in replacing SERPS and in particular the additonal financial burdens this would place on today's workers and the dishonesty of the distinction between state 'pay as you go' schemes and private sector, funded, schemes. Yet the green paper illustrates the ideological and political attractions for the government in pursuing this change regardless. The switch to private (either personal or occupational) pensions, more directly related to actuarial principles and money-purchase, is specifically intended to give as many people as possible a sense that through their pension fund they have a direct interest in increasing the profits of private companies — a personal stake in the success of capitalism. The parallels between this ideology and that of home ownership are made explicit: 'everybody will be able to rely on the fact that their future pension is their own property'.[3]

This strategy attempts to exploit a popular, but mistaken, trust in private savings as opposed to communal welfare. All that differs in reality is the mechanism of transfer. In either case pensioners receive an income derived from employed people: national insurance contributions or taxes are deducted from earnings, paid to the state and then to pensioners; profits are also deducted from workers' potential earnings, paid to share-owning pension funds and then to pensioners. Whatever method of paying for pensions is adopted, the only way of achieving the government's aim of reducing total expenditure on pensions is to reduce pensions, so that the elderly receive a smaller share of national income. Little wonder that the government is not only abolishing SERPS but is also weakening the state requirements for minimum levels of private pensions. The proposals for a 'flexible' retirement age are wholly divisive between those in well-paid secure jobs and those not. 'Flexible' retirement would only be a choice for the well off.

SICKNESS AND DISABILITY

We remarked in chapter six how charity has persisted as an acceptable method of financial support for people with disabilities and that the present lack of a comprehensive system of benefits for people who are sick or have disabilities means that many are forced to rely on means-tested benefits. This would not change under Fowler's proposals — the government's excuse for not addressing the issue is that it is waiting for the results of its current survey of people with disabilities. Consequently people with disabilities would be forced to seek help for special needs from the discretionary social fund, which will be run on charitable principles. Specific reference is made to social fund payments for people moving out of institutions under the 'Care in the Community' programme. The rough justice of the fixed income support premium for those with 'serious health or disablement-related problems' would mean losses for those who need the most additional income. The 'incapacity trap' described in chapter six would be intensified by the relative worsening of benefits for the unemployed.

HOUSING

The process whereby housing expenditure is cut by forcing up rents, pushing more tenants to claim HB and then cutting HB levels is taken a dramatic step further in the Fowler proposals. The government subsidy to local authorities in respect of HB would be massively cut. This would increase the local authorities' contributions to HB by several hundred per cent, in turn putting rates under greater pressure and diverting spending from other local authority programmes. Not content with this, the government would take powers to penalize local authorities which administered HB schemes to the advantage of local residents.

TAXATION

The reviews focus exclusively on social security benefits and completely ignore their relationships to other forms of transfer spending, for example, tax exemptions. The green paper concentrates on shuffling money between those who have very little. Those with plenty would be completely unaffected by the green paper, except as beneficiaries of the consequent tax cuts. The payment of family credit through the wage packet and the alignment of benefit levels for means-tested income support, family credit and HB would be significant moves towards the tax credit type of tax/benefit integration discussed in chapter eight. It would institutionalize the poverty trap (at about 80p in the pound for those in HB only and at over 90p in the pound for those on HB and family credit).[4] The major part of the social security system would be readily adaptable to a comprehensive tax credit system in which the burden of selectivity falls entirely to the claimant.

The Left's Response

The Labour Party has reacted vigorously and aggressively to the Fowler proposals. It has been able to attack effectively the government's political weakness in failing to publish figures in its proposals — with the obvious implication that large cuts are being covered up. However, the Labour Party's position has been essentially a defensive one — retain SERPS, don't cut child benefit, don't scrap additional requirements and single payments, don't cut HB. Apart from Michael Meacher's ill-fated attempts to promote discussions of alternatives there has been little from the Labour Party front bench on what *ought* to be done instead. Consequently it has been forced to argue on a political terrain established by and for the Tories. Arguments of principle have not been raised and the Tories' presentation of the key issues and problems has gone largely unchallenged.

Because the Fowler proposals involve such a definite move to the right, it is tempting for the Labour Party to attempt to occupy some sort of 'middle ground' on social security which does not involve a serious challenge to the status quo. There is serious political danger in doing this, from claimants' and the left's points of view. The defensive response of the Labour Party could entrench traditional, and politically conservative, objectives for the social security system, such as 'the relief of poverty'. Socialist values of fairness, redistribution and social justice will be excluded from the debate on social security.

Objects such as 'the relief of poverty' pose a danger for the left and the labour movement. Once such objectives are accepted for income maintenance, the poor are isolated as a 'problem' to be solved. In turn, this leads inevitably to solutions based on the principles of charity and means tests. The price paid by the poor for their ungenerous 'relief' is one of humiliation, harassment and hopelessness. As long as the organized left is willing to leave them in this state of social isolation, even conceiving of them as a socially isolated problem, the organized left is itself likely to remain in its reciprocal state of political isolation. Attempting to solve this problem by occupying the middle ground of politics is hardly an adequate response to the issues raised by income maintenance.

As far as income maintenance is concerned, the 'politics of the middle ground' is the politics of all the tried, tested and failed solutions of the past: tax breaks for private pensions and owner-occupiers; family dependency for women; earnings-related benefits; insurance; means tests for the poor. The argument we have developed in this book is that these solutions are inegalitarian and don't work to the benefit of those on social security. In addition, they divide those whom the left must unite. They swap the unity and effectiveness of the socialist movement tomorrow for the hope of a bit of peace and quiet today. With mass unemployment, mass poverty and the challenge provided by the government's proposals for reform, that 'peace and quiet' is no longer available. The issue of income maintenance can't be fudged any longer by the left. Socialists must choose between formulating a strategy and practice which seeks to bring workers and non-workers together, or adopting the politics of the middle ground. The latter option means coming to terms with permanent gross poverty and inequality, and allowing the government to pose as radical reformers challenging the institutional conservatism of the left.

In uncompromisingly rejecting this option, we do not advocate abandoning the task of winning over middle-class support for socialism. We reject the facile identification of the 'middle classes' with the political 'middle ground' of Westminster. Many middle-class people clearly share an interest in socialist income maintenance policies: because they are alienated from the undemocratic and inegalitarian nature of British society, because they work within the welfare state, because they have relations or friends dependent on it, because they are concerned about their own security from poverty, because they dislike living in a divided society, and so on. But unlike a strategy to win over the political 'middle ground', winning over such people generally requires putting forward a principled and convincing vision of an alternative to the present mess, and to the Tory plans for change. That conviction can only really be derived from the unity of those without whom the socialist movement cannot ultimately succeed: trade unionists, the low paid and claimants. A strategy for income maintenance is one of the keys to that unity.

Trade Unions and Reform

Fowler's review of social security and the publication of his Green Paper on reform has provoked a new commitment to active campaigning over income maintenance issues. Although at present this commitment is largely limited to Unions within the DHSS — the Civil and Public Servants' Association (CPSA) and the Society for Civil and Public Servants (SCPS) — it represents an important development. The 'Action for Benefits' campaign has brought together these unions with pressure groups at a national level in an aggressive publicity campaign against the proposed cuts. We are still a long way from seeing such cooperation extending directly to claimants themselves at the local level, but the national campaign has been important in creating a campaigning agenda so that such cooperation is a real possibility. However, the 'Action for Benefits' campaign can be criticised for very much the same failings as the response from the Labour Party leadership: indeed the two are obviously closely linked. 'Action for Benefits' has fallen — particularly since the publication of the Green Paper — onto a dangerously uncritical defence of the existing social security system. The positive sounding name of the campaign has not been matched in its practice, which has increasingly become one of campaigning purely for 'no cuts'. The 'Action for Benefits' defence of earnings-related pensions has been forthright, while criticism of the degree of means-testing and stigmatisation inherent in the present system have had to take a back seat.

We have argued in previous chapters that trade unions have a particular problem in responding to the current crisis, because of their traditionally ambivalent attitude to the state's role in income maintenance. They have welcomed state intervention when they have perceived that their members derive benefit from it, for example, Schedule 11 of the Employment Protection Act and the Fair Wages Resolution. Yet trade union leaders have in the past resisted proposals to extend state intervention through a statutory minimum wage; and they have been, at best, indifferent to the effects of the income maintenance system of those currently not in union membership. Some of the ambivalence of trade unions to income maintenance stems from a feeling that they must put the interests of their own members first at all times. Trade unions clearly do have a primary responsibility to their own membership. But, if that responsibility is interpreted in a narrow way, it will ultimately rebound on the members themselves. After all, nearly all of them will have to rely on benefits at some time in their lives — as parents, during sickness or unemployment, and in retirement.

In order to get the full protection of being in trade unions, workers need to be part of a vibrant movement which has convincing and progressive solutions to contemporary problems. In our view, the necessary strength can only be won by abandoning some of the sectional positions on income maintenance of the past. A movement which shirks the difficult task of fighting for the low paid and the non-employed will not gain the moral or numerical force needed to take on the substantial forces of reaction effectively. Fighting on behalf of and with those disadvantaged groups means abandoning the traditional commitments to insurance, earnings-related benefits and tax perks for occupational pension schemes, and beginning an active struggle for minimum wage legislation and decent flat-rate benefits paid without a means test. Many trade union members want the strength and protection of being part of a growing rather than a shrinking movement; and they want the security of an income maintenance system which will provide adequate benefits even if they are made redundant, and which provides those benefits for friends and relations who may not have the privileges which accompany some jobs.

Socialist Radicalism

Obstacles and Arguments for Change

As the Tories have found out, it is one thing to know where you want to go; it is quite another to know how to get there. In their green paper they have mapped out a fairly clear direction for income maintenance: a state scheme based exclusively on a means test; a lower 'poverty floor' especially for the unemployed; the expansion of private provision for the better off. But their ability to achieve such goals with all the attendant political risks seems much more doubtful. For example phasing out child benefit by eroding its real value would take many years and would lead to an annual political row. If the Tories are hitting these obstacles while making their reforms, what obstacles are in the way of a response to the government which proposes reform in the opposite direction?

First of all, 'cost' is not an obstacle. This may seem to be an outlandish statement after six years of Margaret Thatcher telling us that the level of public expenditure is the single problem facing the British economy — an argument repeated in the consultation paper. But it follows logically from the definition of income maintenance that we gave in Chapter 2 and from the distinction between 'transfer' and 'resource' expenditure that we discussed in the last chapter. Because income maintenance is a process of reallocating incomes, it hardly costs the state anything. The costs of administration (resource spending) would almost certainly be reduced by a socialist approach, because the system would be simplified. The obvious right-wing retort is that, even if income maintenance doesn't cost money in resource terms, a reduction in inequality would be costly in terms of lower economic efficiency. We have reviewed in Chapter 3 the central plank of this argument, that a large degree of redistribution would undermine the wage system. We argued that a reduction in the role of cash incentives would entail a re-ordering of the labour system and, in particular, a reversal of the recent trends towards greater hierarchization of the labour market; but that, given such a reorganization, greater equality is compatible with economic efficiency.

Unfortunately, we cannot leave the argument on that happy thought. A major method of reallocation is bound to be through taxation and benefits. Workers often resent the intervention of a third party — the state — taking away through taxation a portion of what they have earned. However, the approach we have adopted in this book would help go a long way towards overcoming this problem: state intervention to guarantee higher incomes (the minimum wage) and lower costs (control of housing costs), rather than the meeting of all needs by state benefits. This is therefore another reason for preferring our approach to any type of 'social credit' or extension of means-tested benefits. It is also important to explain to people the nature of income maintenance as a process of reallocating spending power.

The expectations and perceptions created by the existing system are a second obstacle to genuinely radical income maintenance reform. People have bought homes who wouldn't have been able to afford them without tax breaks — and indeed they may not be able to keep them if those breaks are removed. The pre-budget furore over Nigel Lawson's apparent intention to tax lump-sum pension payments illustrates the moral indignation (or at any rate impression of indignation) which can be generated around this issue. However, we do not believe that this is a permanent obstacle to change. Income maintenance has changed in the past despite the fact that some people have lost as a result; and it will inevitably continue to change. What it means is that a government adopting progressive reforms would need to ensure adequate transitional protection and be sensitive about the timing and presentation of reforms. For example, in Chapter 7, we discuss how simply abolishing mortgage interest tax relief would be very difficult politically. But identifying and freezing the cash level of the government subsidy would erode the real value and lead towards its abolition in a fairer and more politically acceptable manner.

Socialist reforms face a particular difficulty: the people who stand to lose most are the rich and well off. Generally, these people will also be powerful and vocal (some of them own newspapers). They are in a good position to campaign against and actively obstruct reforms which damage their interests. The key to this problem lies not in mollifying the very rich and very powerful — they are unlikely to be mollified by anything short of the extreme inequality which exists today. Instead, we must campaign to undermine the moral legitimacy of the rich, by exposing the scandalous extent of inequality and the lack of fit between the actual contribution the rich make to the economy and the rewards which they grab for themselves.

But no socialist proposals for reform of income maintenance can rely simply on redistributing money from the rich. There aren't enough of them and they aren't rich enough. Inevitably, our proposals involve reducing the incomes of those on average and above-average wages. This is a qualitatively different problem. In contrast to the rich, people on average incomes would receive tangible benefits in exchange, although they would suffer a short-term net reduction of income. In particular, they would have the guarantee of adequate incomes in retirement or if they gave up work for other reasons. Many of them would also be relieved of the burden of financially supporting adults and children currently defined as their 'dependants'.

Indeed because many of the ideas in this book have been directed at re-defining 'need', they would imply a thorough shake-up of income distribution, rather than a simple redistribution on the vertical scale of measurement now used. In cash terms, we advocate a redistribution from men to women, from the childless to parents, from the rich to the poor, from full-time workers to part-time workers, from the employed to the non-employed, and from house-owners to tenants. But the politics of change is much more complicated than a simple cash equation. At least some of those who would lose from reform have to be convinced to support it. It may seem naive to believe that someone with a privilege can be persuaded to surrender it voluntarily. But in our experience many men do believe that women should have financial independence. Many people without children believe that the state should ensure that children are adequately supported. Many well-paid workers reject the politics of mass unemployment and the poverty which accompanies it.

What is needed is confidence in the practicality of a fairer and more rational method of income distribution. In previous chapters we have attempted to describe a coherent vision of such a method. We have attempted to derive this vision from a consideration of the socialist principles of income maintenance. For this reason, we have consistently rejected the principle of 'selectivity' as it is applied to individuals in need through means-testing. We have tried to replace it with a principle of selectivity applied to public investment, subsidy and services. Ultimately, the attractiveness of such an approach will rest not on the simple question of cash gainers and losers, but on the question of whether people can be convinced to struggle for greater control over the economic and social conditions which shape their lives. It sounds like an easy argument to win, but it means reversing the retreat into a philosophy of individual blame and personal aggrandizement. The message of socialism is a message of hope, but, as such, it depends on defeating the anarchic pessimism of the Thatcherite philosophy.

Getting Round the Obstacles

Whatever the conditions in which progressive reform may become a possibility, it is clear that it will depend on a strong alliance — of trade unionists, unorganized workers and the non-employed — with a clear idea of the direction which change must take. We should not be pessimistic about the potential strength of such an alliance. In terms of sheer numbers, we should remember that it would make up a large majority of the population. There are currently around 11 million workers in trade unions. There are about 8.3 million low-paid workers and a further 7 million people living on supplementary benefit. There are over 10 million people of pensionable age. Probably at least 5 million people are seriously disabled. There are overlaps between these categories, and we cannot assume that all the people in each group can be won over to support change. But figures like these are enough to indicate that it is not the arithmetic of a popular majority which is the primary obstacle to progress. Tory policies have massively increased the numbers of these people who have a direct stake in improvements in income maintenance.

One of the major obstacles is the lack of a practice, among these quite diverse groups who stand to gain from change, of actually working and campaigning together around income maintenance issues. But it is possible to discern definite signs of hope. Some unions are actively adopting a more radical approach on income maintenance. The National Union of Public Employees has campaigned strongly for a statutory minimum wage and there are signs that other unions may at last follow suit. The General, Municipal, Boilermakers and Allied Trades Union has begun, however belatedly, to attempt to recruit the unemployed. It is clear that DHSS unions and claimants do have a common interest in opposing staff and benefit cuts and as we have said above the 'Action for Benefits' campaign has been an important initiative in this direction. At a local level, the activities of the Specialist Claims Control groups have acted as a catalyst, bringing unions and claimants together. Largely as a result of the government reviews there is also a nascent awakening of interest in social security in the Labour Party. At a policy level, the Labour Campaign for Social Security has for the first time seriously raised the possibility of an alternative to the old 'back-to-Beveridge' approach.

The growth of the welfare rights movement in response to mass unemployment and poverty is also a positive development. There is, of course, a danger of professionalization; the case of social work shows how easy it is for a supposedly radical profession to be largely coopted by the state into a role of social control. The world of advice work, in particular Citizens' Advice Bureaux, has traditionally been dominated by a paternalistic rather than progressive approach. However, some Labour local authorities have recently demonstrated a commitment to a more political form of welfare rights work by employing workers with a campaigning role. These workers have often been able to carry out a process of educating some local Labour politicians and many community activists about the politics of social security.

Most fundamentally, mass unemployment and poverty, experience of the effect of Tory welfare policies and the prospect of major cuts in the benefit system as a result of government proposals have all combined to awaken a much greater degree of public interest in income maintenance issues. We have found through our own work that there is now a hunger for knowledge about income maintenance, particularly among claimants themselves, which wasn't there five or ten years ago. The confidence to acquire such knowledge is a prerequisite of the confidence to campaign for a better system. Educating the public about income maintenance, involving more people in campaigns and winning the Labour and trade union leaderships to socialist policies on income maintenance, these are the crucial tasks in the process of building an alliance capable of achieving real progress. More people than ever before are gaining first-hand experience of the social security system and what they are finding is a system in crisis, presided over by a government which wishes to make still further cuts. This has created massive disaffection with the current system and a unique opportunity to win support for the type of clear alternative perspective that only a socialist approach provides.

Campaigning Themes

Up to a point people can be united around minimalist demands: do not cut staff; do not cut benefits; raise child benefit; give the long-term rate to the unemployed. But such positions are unlikely ever to lead to major changes. They would never inspire mass support because they are so insipid. And it is in the nature of change that it is usually implemented by politicians and civil servants who are not necessarily very committed to any particular direction of change. If politicians are not given instructions by the wider movement to which they should be responsible, the prospects for radical change are slight. Change is not likely to be brought about by the ifs, buts and maybes, and some-of-us-think statements which currently riddle left discussion of income maintenance.

The problem is illustrated by the analogies between the current response to Norman Fowler's consultative paper and the positions taken in response to a less wide-ranging reform considered by the last Labour government. In 1978 there was a review of supplementary benefit initiated by the Labour government, which resulted in the *Social Assistance* report.[5] At the time, many activists said that the current system was terrible, but that we ought to defend it because it was under attack. Opposition united around a 'no cuts' stand, with the intention, when the campaign was over, of sitting down at leisure to discuss a socialist way forward. Indeed genuine efforts were made in the following years to have such discussions, and this book owes its genesis to those discussions. Nevertheless, seven years on, activists are again saying in response to the Tory review, 'We haven't quite worked out our position yet. The current system is terrible, but it's better than what the Tories want. Let us defend what we've got and talk about the alternatives later.' We won't defeat the Tories with apologetic statements such as these — they're the ones who should be making the apologies.

Take the vexed question of the state earnings-related pensions scheme (SERPS) for example. It's inevitable that because the Tories want to get rid of it as a means of cutting spending on pensions, many people will be pushed into defending it, even those who acknowledge that it is inegalitarian and a bad use of the money available to spend on pensions. But really we shouldn't have to be on the defensive in this way. The socialist alternative to SERPS — decent flat-rate pensions for all and a withdrawal of tax subsidies to private pensions — are far more threatening to the Tories than is SERPS itself. It is they who should be clinging on to it, not the left. Had the left mounted a socialist critique of it in the past, it is much less likely that the Tories would be proposing getting rid of it: they would be more fearful of breaking the two-party consensus on pensions for fear of what a future Labour government might put in its place. It is time that socialist criticisms of earnings-related pensions were clearly put, if only as a counterweight to right wing propaganda.

The area of individual assessment is another where the right should be on the defensive, because of the weakness of their argument. The idea of basing assessment on the family unit is plainly paternalistic and demeaning to women, suggesting as it does that women do not have the right to be treated as independent individuals. Opposition to individual assessment because of the cost is thoroughly hypocritical as well; it usually argues that women are already adequately supported financially within the family and that supporting them adequately through income maintenance would be 'too expensive'. If married women already have adequate incomes, they should be treated as adults and receive the money directly. If they don't have adequate incomes, isn't it about time they did?

A similar mist of hypocrisy surrounds the issue of child support. This, we are told, is a 'family responsibility'. The state should only intervene where there is genuine poverty and should 'target' resources on those in greatest need. People choose to have children; let them pay for them. Are the Tories telling us that children are just another commodity in the 'enterprise culture'? Like hire purchase agreements on cookers and settees, you shouldn't have taken them on if you can't afford them. Yet this very enterprise culture has no answer to the problem of child support. We are told that Britain's economic future depends on driving down wages to the lowest possible level. Clearly that is the level at which a single person without dependants can survive. The Tories will not force employers to pay a 'family wage' so that workers have wages high enough to support their families and indeed are proposing to further subsidise low-paying employers by the backdoor — through the family credit scheme. People are fed up with this kind of Tory hypocrisy.

Campaigns must also focus on the Tory tax hand-outs. As we have seen, these go in vast quantities to the rich and are completely ignored in the green paper. But tax handouts also go in lesser quantities to home owners and workers covered by occupational pension schemes. Many of these people can be persuaded that they stand to gain from the elimination of the irrationality and injustice of these concessions. Because a lot of people have made a lot of money out of tax concessions, the idea has been promoted that the market can meet housing need. Yet, in reality, occupational pension funds chiefly advantage a minority — those with well-paid jobs; and the housing market is an irrational process which hurts as many people as it helps, fails to meet need and relies on massive state subsidy for survival.

The whole issue of 'community care' for the disabled and elderly is another area where the right can be placed on the defensive. Both groups traditionally provoke the sentimental sympathy of Tory politicians and supporters. Recently the Tories have 'discovered' that these groups would generally be better and more happily cared for in their own communities. The Tories are happy with one consequence of this discovery: they can set about closing all the long-stay hospitals and homes, sacking the workers and chucking out the residents. But the Tories do not wish to plough the resources back into community care. They do not wish to provide the disabled with a decent income so that they can live independently. And they do not wish to provide adequate income support for carers. Instead they propose to provide 'help' through a glorified state charity — the social fund.

It is also time that the offensive was taken on the issue of racism in social security. As we have seen, the present system discriminates against ethnic minorities through residence rules, earnings-related benefits and a range of administrative measures which lead to the harassment of black claimants. The proposed 'presence test' for income support will worsen their position. The campaign for a non-racist system must be seen as a key element of all the other issues which are tackled.

The weakness of the Tory idea of 'enterprise culture' can be exploited in the argument against means-testing. The Tories tell us that state hand-outs are a bad thing and that individuals should be able to survive without them. Yet they indiscriminately subsidize employers who pay starvation wages, by supplementing those wages with a whole range of demeaning means tests. There is a socialist concept of enterprise too: it is a process of production and wealth creation in which all employers meet their responsibilities to their workers and their consumers as well as to themselves. The first step in enforcing such responsibilities is the imposition of a statutory minimum wage.

In all of these areas campaigns must respond to the government's proposals by putting forward the possibility of a state benefit system which meets needs without tests of means or contributions, guaranteeing dignity for claimants and workers. We have argued that the best way in which that can be achieved is through a system of individually assessed positional and cost-related benefits, progressive and comprehensive taxation, and a minimum wage. Others will doubtless disagree. Let us at least start the debate about a better way forward, rather than continually looking over our shoulders for the best path of retreat.

Notes

1. DHSS, The Reform of Social Security, 4 vols, London 1985.
2. DHSS, Volume 2 paragraph 4.46.
3. DHSS, Volume 2 paragraph 1.67.
4. These estimates of the combined withdrawal rates for tax and benefits assume income tax of 30 per cent, national insurance of 8 per cent and a minimum pension contribution of 2 per cent all on gross income. Once these are deducted, housing benefit is withdrawn at the rate of 70 per cent and we assume a family credit withdrawal rate of 50 per cent (equal to family income supplement) from the remaining income. These give a combined withdrawal rate of 30 + 8 + 2 + 42 + 9 = 91 per cent.
5. DHSS, *Social Assistance: A Review of Supplementary Benefit*, London 1978.

Index